for wine &

wandering—

Cheers!

Lynda & Larry

"While there's often a disconnect between spirituality and celebration, in *The Soul of Wine* Gisela Kreglinger invites us into the vineyard to experience the abundance of God. Written by the daughter of a German vintner, the book heralds cultural healing through God's gift of wine."

Sandra McCracken, singer-songwriter and recording artist in Nashville

"Anyone who loves wine knows that it is the world's most spiritual beverage—a beverage steeped in mystery and transformation. In this deeply personal account, Gisela Kreglinger explores how wine can evoke the divine in everyday life. Kreglinger shares thoughtful musings, examples, and ideas that spiritual wine lovers will find captivating and affirming."

Karen MacNeil, author of *The Wine Bible*

"Here is a wine book that is at once wise, refreshing, and delightful: wise because it draws on a lifetime's Christian reflection on wine and on the wisdom of Scripture and tradition, refreshing because it sets the reader free from all the absurd competitiveness and anxiety of wine snobbery and restores wine to its rightful place at the heart of inclusion and community, and delightful because Gisela Kreglinger addresses the reader with such clarity, charm, and style. This book not only celebrates the soul of wine, it also speaks deeply to the soul of its readers."

Malcolm Guite, Girton College, Cambridge

"Spirituality and wine are two realms that have been too often reserved for an elite class of devotees and drinkers. To me, this is a tragedy as I consider the fruit of the vine to be one of God's greatest gifts, and artfully made wine to be one of the most profound and pleasurable collaborations between God and humans. I am thankful that in *The Soul of Wine* Gisela Kreglinger is making both soul and wine accessible and inviting to the expert and beginner alike. Cheers!"

Adam McHugh, wine tour guide and sommelier, author of *The Listening Life*

"When I was growing up, my father and two uncles were preachers. For communion, Welch's grape juice was served. Such blasphemous deprivation might explain why I ended up in the business of fine wines. What a joy to find a book that combines divinity and *vinity* (to coin a word). Believers and nonbelievers will gain new respect for the fermented fruit of the vine. A gem of a book, it is a great read and makes me wonder why some modern religions treat wine as a sin when the Bible so clearly considers it God's gift to man and womankind."
Kermit Lynch, wine importer and author of *Adventures on the Wine Route*

"I read *The Soul of Wine* with increasing delight and ever deeper emotion. This book offers wisdom not just about wine, but about our souls as well—about the joy, grief, and beauty that shape all of our stories, and that are so intertwined with the making of wine. It will help me drink more slowly and more meaningfully not just from my next glass of wine, but from life itself."
Andy Crouch, author of *Culture Making: Recovering Our Creative Calling*

"As much as wine delights and communes its drinkers, it intimidates and divides some as well. In *The Soul of Wine*, Kreglinger dispels the myth that wine appreciation requires a distinguished palate or an elite vocabulary. Rather she presents wine as a simple gift from God that, when stewarded well, offers a glimpse of creation as it is meant to be."
Kendall Vanderslice, author of *We Will Feast: Rethinking Dinner, Worship, and the Community of God*

"Wine saturates the Scriptures. God gave wine 'to gladden the hearts of humanity,' to deepen our understanding and celebration of a redeemed life. Yet many of us, to be 'spiritual' have abstained. Gisela wisely and beautifully shows us a better way. *The Soul of Wine* opens our eyes, our mouths, and our appetites to learn and taste all that God has so lavishly given. I'm feasting and rejoicing more fully because of it."
Leslie Leyland Fields, author/editor of *The Spirit of Food: 34 Writers on Feasting and Fasting Toward God*

THE SOUL
OF
Wine

SAVORING THE
GOODNESS OF GOD

GISELA H. KREGLINGER

An imprint of InterVarsity Press
Downers Grove, Illinois

InterVarsity Press
P.O. Box 1400, Downers Grove, IL 60515-1426
ivpress.com
email@ivpress.com

InterVarsity Press® is the book-publishing division of InterVarsity Christian Fellowship/USA®, a movement of students and faculty active on campus at hundreds of universities, colleges, and schools of nursing in the United States of America, and a member movement of the International Fellowship of Evangelical Students. For information about local and regional activities, visit intervarsity.org.

Scripture quotations, unless otherwise noted, are from the New Revised Standard Version of the Bible, copyright 1989 by the Division of Christian Education of the National Council of the Churches of Christ in the USA. Used by permission. All rights reserved.

While any stories in this book are true, some names and identifying information may have been changed to protect the privacy of individuals.

Cover design and image composite: David Fassett
Interior design: Daniel van Loon
Images: bunch of grapes: © Creativ Studio Heinemann / Getty Images
   red wine stain: © winvic / iStock / Getty Images Plus
   single red wine splash: © Oleksii Pollishchuk / iStock / Getty Images Plus
   cardboard texture background: © Katsumi Murouchi / Moment Collection / Getty Images

ISBN 978-0-8308-4584-2 (print)
ISBN 978-0-8308-4383-1 (digital)

Printed in the United States of America ∞

InterVarsity Press is committed to ecological stewardship and to the conservation of natural resources in all our operations. This book was printed using sustainably sourced paper.

Library of Congress Cataloging-in-Publication Data
A catalog record for this book is available from the Library of Congress.

P   *25 24 23 22 21 20 19 18 17 16 15 14 13 12 11 10 9 8 7 6 5 4 3 2 1*

Y   *37 36 35 34 33 32 31 30 29 28 27 26 25 24 23 22 21 20 19*

CONTENTS

In memory of

JAN

and

EUGENE PETERSON

For you have given me wings to fly

CHAPTER ONE

SENSING GOD IN WINE

May God give you of the dew of heaven,
and of the fatness of the earth,
and plenty of grain and wine.

GENESIS 27:28

I have always loved the world of wine as we experienced it on a small family-run winery. My childhood growing up on a winery did not make me into a vintner though. Two of my sisters embraced that blessed vocation. I chose a vocation with a similar feel to it. I wanted to be a theologian, working in God's vineyard, and it still surprises me to see how profoundly the world of faith and the world of wine are interwoven.

Wine is an astonishing gift to humanity, and I firmly believe that wine can help uncork a more full-bodied Christian spirituality in our midst and enrich our lives around the Table. At their best, choice wines can evoke a great sense of awe and wonder within us. They hint at a Presence among us that is so full of splendor, magnificence, and beauty that we creatures of dust and breath would be utterly overwhelmed if we encountered this Presence face to face. We earthlings only seem to get glimpses of it here and there.

> "I will restore the fortunes
> of my people Israel,
> and they shall rebuild the
> ruined cities and inhabit them;
> they shall plant vineyards
> and drink their wine,
> and they shall make
> gardens and eat their fruit.
> I will plant them
> upon their land,
> and they shall never
> again be plucked up."
>
> AMOS 9:14-15 (ABOUT
> THE MESSIANIC AGE)

Since ancient times people have believed that wine is imbued with spiritual meaning and can become a mediator between heaven and earth, evoking divine presence. The Greeks believed in the wine god Dionysus, the Romans in Bacchus, and the Etruscans in Fufluns. The Jews believe God gave them wine to make glad their hearts, and Christians celebrate the Lord's Supper with bread and wine. Once upon a time all of these different faith traditions believed that a mysterious presence hovered over the powerful process of fermentation, urging it on with divine purpose.

One of the great gifts of my childhood is that I grew up with a family and culture that celebrated wine as a gift from God and allowed this divine beverage to transform our mundane moments into beautiful encounters, sometimes imbued with heavenly bliss.

JESUS AND WINE

Growing up on a winery, the great abundance of the earth mingled with my experiences at church, where I heard and listened to the marvelous stories of Jesus of Nazareth. I remember vividly the story of the tax collector Zacchaeus, a wealthy man who wanted to get a glimpse of the great prophet who had come into town. So Zacchaeus ran ahead and climbed a tree to make sure he got to see Jesus when he walked by. Zacchaeus was a wretched man, but he was hungry and thirsty for more. Jesus saw him in the tree, called him by name, and invited himself to dinner at Zacchaeus's house—just like that. How did Jesus know his name?

I had no doubt, listening to this story as a little girl, that Zacchaeus would have provided a banquet for Jesus with only the best food and wine. Just like my dad, he would have gone down into the wine cellar himself to select a wide range of choice wines for this honorable guest, wines he would only pull out for special occasions. They would have talked late into the night and bonded over food and wine. At the end of the evening, Zacchaeus's life was transformed. Jesus' loving and accepting presence had touched him so deeply that this once-greedy man gave half of his wealth away, and he was unburdened and ready to enter the kingdom of heaven.

Jesus performed miracles to pull away the veil that keeps our eyes and ears, our noses and tongues from sensing God's presence among us. In Jesus' life, his words and deeds both great and small, in the way he encountered and touched people, through his suffering, death, and resurrection, we see into the very heart of God, our loving Father. His life-spending Spirit continues to revitalize and green even the most barren places of our lives and communities if we allow him to move among us. He is not forceful or overbearing but woos us into his presence like a lover does his beloved bride.

First things and last things are important in a person's life and ministry. They announce and mark and signal to us what a person values and wants us to remember and be grounded in. Writers give witness to what they have heard and seen about people who changed the course of history, and we need to pay careful attention to their words, especially as they tell us about those first and last things these people have done. This is no less true for the Gospels, which give witness to Jesus Christ, the Son of the living God.

> *"I tell you, I will never again drink of this fruit of the vine until that day when I drink it new with you in my Father's kingdom."*
>
> JESUS THE MESSIAH,
> MATTHEW 26:29

In the Gospel of John we learn that Jesus' first miracle was turning water into wine at a Jewish peasant wedding where the host had run out of wine. His last miracle was supernaturally providing an abundance of fish for his ragamuffin fishermen followers, including Peter, who had betrayed him three times.

Fruit of the earth and fruit of the sea become places where God reveals his glorious and loving presence among us, feeding and nurturing us in body, soul, and spirit. Jesus even cooks some fish by the beach *before* his disciples are able to haul that great catch onto the shore.

Our harvests, whether in wine or fish, in words and deeds, will only ever add a little to that great abundance that God has provided for us both in the fruits of the earth and the resurrected Christ, who is the first fruit of all of creation.

THE GIFT OF FIVE SENSES

Not too long ago I took part in the Bay Area Book Festival in Berkeley, California. My book *The Spirituality of Wine* had just come out, and the organizers had assigned me a booth located on "Inspiration Row," sandwiched in between Hare Krishnas and Buddhists. It was a fascinating experience, and I was eager to get acquainted with my neighbors. The Hare Krishna couple had brought candies and offered them freely to those passing by. Once the candy was accepted, the Hare Krishna couple invited the visitors to learn more about their faith tradition. They had a book they would open to help them explain.

I was intrigued. I wanted to learn about them and during a quiet spell went over and introduced myself. The lady kindly opened her book and showed me an image of a cart pulled by five horses. She explained that the five horses represent the five senses: seeing, hearing, touching, smelling, and tasting. As the picture showed, we must learn to reign in the five senses because they always want to lead us astray, away from the true spiritual path. If someone offers you some ice cream, she explained, you want more and can't stop. *Yes, that sounded familiar!* I thought. She believed that the senses are deceptive and lead us astray. We must not trust them but learn instead to control them. As you progress on the spiritual path, you have to learn how to reign in the senses and fight against their appetites. I had never thought of it before, but fundamentally, for the Hare Krishna, the five senses are bad, and we must do all we can to control them in order to ascend to a higher spiritual realm.

There, I had a little bit of a revelation. I suddenly realized that most religions practiced today believe that the five senses contribute little to true spiritual enlightenment, and in order to progress in the spiritual life we must detach ourselves from physical pleasure and withdraw to the spiritual within. It dawned on me then that the Jewish and Christian faiths are the only faith traditions as far as I am aware that believe the five senses are a gift from God, a gift to be embraced, treasured, and celebrated. And yet even within the Christian tradition there is still a profound suspicion toward the senses of touch, smell, and taste, and how they might aid us in our pursuit of sensing God's presence among us.

We need to rediscover and affirm our God-given senses as the only way through which we can come to know and sense God's presence with us. God gave wine to make glad the hearts of humanity. Wine has a unique way of helping us forge new alliances, strengthen bonds of friendships, and build community. It connects us to the earth, inspires us toward creativity, and invites us to linger in the present moment, both secular and sacred. Savoring a well-crafted glass of wine can move us to commune with God and embrace the joy that comes from receiving this gift with receptive hearts, noses, and tongues.

REDISCOVERING WINE

All the great theologians and church reformers wrote about and celebrated wine as a gift from God. Up until the nineteenth century all Christian traditions served wine in the Lord's Supper. And yet in today's Christian culture, there is little witness to this rich interweaving of wine, feasting, and redemptive living. Wine just isn't talked about. I believe this has created a void in our culture, and we have given over to the secular world the task of determining the meaning of wine for us. I think that's quite tragic. Why?

Many can't see and don't experience those moments of grace when a lovely and delectable wine softens the hard places within and opens us up to those around us. That's particularly heart-wrenching because at no other time in history have we had such easy access to great and wonderful wines from around the world right at our local wine stores.

> *"The earth also shall yield its fruit ten-thousandfold and on each vine there shall be a thousand branches, and each branch shall produce a thousand clusters, and each cluster produce a thousand grapes, and each grape produce a cor of wine. And those who have hungered shall rejoice: more over, also, they shall behold marvels every day."*
>
> 2 BARUCH 29:5-6 (ABOUT THE MESSIANIC KINGDOM)

North Americans in particular are rediscovering wine, and it is quickly becoming a powerful cultural force in our midst. The aftermath of the Prohibition could only last so long, and on a broad scale people are discovering that wine is a fantastic drink. Wineries are popping up all over the place. Wine shops and wine bars have added color and sophistication to downtown areas and residential neighborhoods, and even at airports fast-food chains give way to a more demanding and liberated clientele that has become increasingly dissatisfied with junk food. It's an exciting development, but I feel there is something missing, something important.

THE CHALLENGES OF CONTEMPORARY WINE TALK

With the emergence of a new and young wine culture has come a way of talking about wine I find both intriguing and enlightening, but also unsettling and restrictive. Over the last fifty years or so a new guild of wine writers, wine educators, and sommeliers has emerged who take their work seriously. You can learn much from them. However, they have emerged out of a highly competitive consumer culture, and they perpetuate ways of talking about wine that quickly pull us into a competitive, elitist, and perhaps exclusive way of talking about wine. It can easily make us feel inadequate, ignorant, and overwhelmed. That's not fun, and that's not how it was meant to be. It goes against the grain of what love and grace are all about and what gifts are for.

When talk about wine becomes a barrier for you to be able to enter the world of wine and explore wine on your own terms and enjoy it, then something important has gotten lost. The door is shut for many who would otherwise be quite interested in exploring wine. Ultimately, no one can capture the beauty of a well-crafted wine in language. Words help for sure, but they can only hint at the beauty and complexity we experience in a well-crafted wine. Wines at their best make us marvel and instill in us a sense of awe for what this earth is capable of bringing forth. They lift us out of the mundane to a place of wonder and give us a glimpse into the very heart of what it means to be alive in this world. There is mystery in wine.

I am concerned that many of you, perhaps new to the world of wine, feel so intimidated and overwhelmed by it all that you think it's not for you. You might walk into a supermarket or a wine shop, or look at the long wine list in a fancy restaurant with names that you will never be able to pronounce, and think it's best left to the experts and wine enthusiasts. *It's not for me.* But God gave wine to make glad the hearts of humanity, and to miss out on this great gift and the joy and conviviality it can bring is a great loss.

It is freeing when you can look back in history and learn how different cultures and writers have understood wine. It opens up a vision that liberates you to consider a wider world and embrace values that are perhaps more welcoming and inclusive. When Benedictine nuns first began planting vines along the river Main in our region of Germany, they had a particular way of understanding wine. They ingested the Bible and the Rule of St. Benedict daily, and this perspective shaped their vision and values. They saw wine as a gift from God and crafted it for the celebration of the Lord's Supper, for their own nourishment, and to share it with those around them. Both the Bible and the Rule of St. Benedict stress the importance of hospitality and taking care of the sick, poor, and vulnerable of society. To share the wine they crafted with guests, pilgrims, the sick, and the poor was fundamental to their vision of the Christian life.

Even fourteen hundred years later, Christians still uphold those beliefs and values, and yet when it comes to wine, we've allowed the secular world to define what wine is for. Wine and wine talk has become a way to differentiate yourself from others and help you to secure a sense of identity built on your education, knowledge, and financial success. It has tendencies to be competitive, exclusive, and elitist. I think it's time to reclaim wine as a gift from God and re-define its meaning on our own terms, away from the pressures of the highly competitive consumer societies that seem to haunt us wherever we go.

ENJOYING WINE AS A GIFT FROM GOD

While wine has long been an integral part of European culture, the ordinary wine drinker does not know much about wine. Traditionally, they only drank their local wines and didn't know much about those particular local wines either. It was part of their culture just like their local cheese and bread. And they enjoyed the wine without the pressure to become a sophisticated wine consumer. That's still the case with most wine drinkers where I come from in Franconia, where wine has been cultivated since the Romans came. It was and is just part of life and part of *joie de vivre*—the enjoyment of life. These innocent times are gone.

We have to learn to maneuver our way around this ever-changing and complex world of wine where the wine-marketing experts fiercely compete for our attention and want to submit us to their talk about wine.

I have written *The Soul of Wine* to help you rediscover wine as a spiritual and cultural gift. We must reclaim wine as a gift from God and allow it to bring joy and conviviality into our midst. Wine was never meant just for a small and elite group of well-to-do people but is a gift from God to us all. We can and should learn together how wine can help us reconnect with God, one another, and creation. Wine can reenchant the world for us and help us fall in love with it all over again. There is a good reason why Jesus' first miracle was turning water into wine. Few created things can hint at the glory of the heavenly wedding banquet like a choice wine can.

I would like to introduce you to the world of wine sip by sip, help you shed any sense of intimidation that you might have, and help you embrace this world with a sense of curiosity and wonder. I want you to come alongside me and let me by your guide. Let's have some fun while we explore this together and keep those at bay who seek to intimidate us by their sometimes outlandish and elitist wine talk. Let the convivial embrace begin.

This book is about rediscovering the gift of wine for what it was meant to be and do: reveal glimpses of God's incredible love, generosity, and benevolence toward us. We have let this gift fall by the wayside, and the secular world now defines the meaning of wine for us. It eclipses the superabundant generosity of God, who always desires to give us more than we need, even wine. We are more than survivors in this world; our lives were never meant to be just about water and bread but also about wine and wild-caught fish.

CHAPTER TWO

A JOYFUL JOURNEY
TO A SPIRITUAL GIFT

God brings forth wine to gladden the human heart.

PSALM 104:15 (AUTHOR'S PARAPHRASE)

ince ancient times people have understood wine as a mediator between heaven and earth, the sacred and the secular, the extraordinary and the ordinary, and even a place of revelation. And yet it still comes as a surprise to many that wine should have played such an important role in people's spiritual experiences, especially in the Jewish and Christian faith traditions.

This amnesia is a heartrending loss because the Bible is saturated with talk about wine. It's the most talked about food, and there are nearly a thousand references to wine and wine-related themes in these sacred Scriptures. The psalmist writes that God "bring[s] forth food from the earth, and wine to gladden the human heart" (Psalm 104:14-15). That's an astonishing pronouncement.

We are supposed to take pleasure in wine and lean into a life of joy as part of our spiritual journey? Yes, that is what it says.

We all know that joy and gladness are hard to come by in our world, and to reject the gifts of God that are to bring us joy seems like a deeply flawed approach to the spiritual life. We are in desperate need of more joy in our world, so why abandon one of the most wonderful and delicious gifts from God? It doesn't really make sense, does it?

> *"Wine drunk at the proper time brings joy, cheerfulness and conviviality."*
>
> **BEN SIRA (C. 200 BC), JEWISH WISDOM TEACHER**

Have you ever wondered why we don't hear much about what Jesus would eat and drink or how much Jesus enjoyed his regular cup of wine? Did you know that he enjoyed wine, food, and dinner parties so much that his fellow Jews accused him of being a glutton and a drunkard? I guess we don't talk about this part of Jesus' life much because we don't think it's that important. Or perhaps it doesn't fit into our picture of who Jesus was, and so we quietly pass over these seemingly unimportant, unnecessary, and perhaps even embarrassing details.

Usually, we hear about what Jesus said and did—the miracles he performed and what others have written about what he said and did. From that we are supposed to know what we should say and do. Most of the teaching I've heard settles on the moral level. It's about right and wrong, good and bad, what we ought to do and how we ought to behave.

When we come to passages in Scripture that can't be pulled down to that level, we tend to pass them by. They're just pure ornamentation. Protestants like me certainly have done that with Jesus' transfiguration. It's an unusual story for sure. It's a story of pure bliss and beauty and revelation without immediate moral implications. Orthodox Christians devote a whole day to celebrate Jesus' transfiguration and meditate on it extensively through their icons and art. We Protestants tend to ignore it—at least this is my experience. It seems that when we can't draw a moral from a story, we don't know what to do with it.

WINE RULES

Perhaps the only thing you have heard about wine is that it is dangerous—or worse, that wine is bad and that you should steer away from it. In Christian circles we've often reduced the subject of wine to questions of good and bad. More recently, the "wine experts" have made knowing about wine highly competitive and exclusive. Talk about wine has become so convoluted that it feels to many of us like an impenetrable maze. No wonder that too many still have ambivalent feelings about wine. Some still wonder, *Is it right or wrong to drink wine? Wouldn't it be better if all abstained?* Others might think, *The wine world is by far too complicated, sophisticated, and elitist for me*—and they conclude that wine is just not for them. That's unfortunate because wine is supposed to be for everyone.

The other day I went to get a wine glass out of the cabinet to have a small glass of wine while I wrapped up a long writing day. It was just before six p.m., and my friend Noranne saw me get the wine glass and said, "Oh, you naughty girl!" We both laughed, but there was this underlying sense that I was doing something forbidden. I don't think many church cultures are at all clear about how they feel about wine, and there are still too many unspoken prejudices and rules against it.

Our relationship with wine is far from being healed and restored. The most outrageous sermon I have heard about the wedding feast of Cana was when a Baptist theologian preached on it and argued that the wine really didn't matter at all in the story. What did matter was that Jesus revealed his sovereign power. I looked

> *Our relationship with wine is far from being healed and restored.*

around the room and saw all these eager students take in this misreading of the text. They seemed to swallow it hook, line, and sinker. It made me sad and angry.

Why are we so obsessed with Jesus' power and sovereignty that we forget to notice beauty and deny ourselves his extravagant generosity? I found, and still find, all this quite puzzling.

PILGRIMS

Benedictine nuns began planting vines and crafting wine in the region where my family lives as early as the sixth century. They believed that wine was a gift from God and inseparable from the good news they were bringing to these wild and unruly barbarian tribes of Europe. After all, they needed wine for the celebration of the Eucharist. We have fourteen hundred years of unbroken belief in the goodness of the earth, the soil, and of course wine as part of our spiritual heritage.

Everything we did as a family had to do with the sun and the rain, heat and cold, water and soil, digging into the earth and planting vines, harvesting grapes and watching this amazing miracle of grape juice slowly but surely turning into wine. Smells of organic soil, fermenting grape juice, and fragrant wine have haunted me all my life long. These smells are impressed on my imagination, and the memories are vivid and make me feel glad—even giddy. I grew up with a fundamental sense that this earth is good and that wine is a special gift from God to bring us joy and deepen our experience of joy.

Year in and year out my family has been concerned with—or perhaps it's more honest to say obsessed over—this one thing: to craft wine and hope that it will bring joy and conviviality to our customers. We all knew that this joy is not just ours to grasp but is something that we need to cultivate and protect for generations yet to be born. My dad, who isn't a very religious person, would turn into a religious zealot whenever it came to the earth and the soil and our responsibility to take care of it.

People come and go every day from far and near to our tasting room to sample wine. But they don't just come to sample wine. While their mouths and noses are attuned to sniff and smell, to taste and savor, they also want to talk. They linger. Our tasting room invites people to stay for a little while.

Often our customers want to talk about the wine but also about the vineyards, the soil, the weather, the new vintage, and the struggles and joys we had in crafting it. They also ask about our family, and we ask about their families. We have known many of our customers for a long time. Beyond the tasting and savoring, the getting and spending, there is perhaps something else people are searching for.

Though pilgrimages have come back into fashion again, most people I know go on holidays to recover from their stressful lives in the city. Wineries and tasting rooms have increasingly become holiday destinations. Many of our customers are on vacation. You might wonder why that is.

What are people looking for when they go to a winery? Can't they just pick up a bottle of wine at the supermarket and save them-

> *"A book of Verses underneath the Bough, A Jug of Wine, a Loaf of Bread—and Thou Beside me singing in the Wilderness— Oh, Wilderness were Paradise now!"*
>
> OMAR KHAYYAM (1048–1131), PERSIAN POET AND PHILOSOPHER

selves all the trouble of traveling to wineries and tasting rooms? What is it about these places that draws us into their spell?

I've watched this enchantment all my life, and I have often wondered about it. Something about wine has captured the imagination of people throughout the ages. Somehow wine casts a spell on those who are open and receptive to its wondrous and mysterious allures.

I believe that wine has such a spell on people because it is a unique gift that opens our lives to greater and more mysterious realities. It hints at splendors and beauty and joy we often don't notice in the hustle and bustle of our daily lives. For those who see with eyes of faith, wine becomes a spiritual gift, imbued with spiritual meaning. Wine was never meant to be just another beverage. In the Bible wine's role is to open our lives to the Giver of all good things, God himself. The beauty and complexity of wine hints at a reality much greater than what our eyes can see, our hands can touch, our tongues can taste, and our noses can smell. Wine hints at the unfathomable generosity of our Creator, who invites us into his presence to linger and to be filled with his love and grace and joy.

CHAPTER THREE

WE ARE THIRSTY

"You have kept the good wine until now." Jesus did this,
the first of his signs, in Cana of Galilee, and revealed his glory.

JOHN 2:10-11

*O*ur family's winery is happily situated in a small medieval
village. That means there is really no room for a garden in the
village. In medieval times people built the houses close together and
surrounded the village with a stone wall to protect it from invaders.
The gardens are mostly outside the village along the river Main. It's
only a short walk to the outskirts of the village, and it takes just a
few minutes to get to our rather larger-than-life garden.

As we open the gate to the garden, we first pass the chicken
coop, once populated by rather feisty and industrious chickens.

It now hosts three aging geese. My family first got them when my sister's three children were still little. Each of the children got to name one of the geese. As the children have grown up, the geese have grown old. They remind us that not all of life has to be industrious and productive and useful. Their sole purpose is to be there, blissfully unaware of what is happening to the rest of the world, and to keep us company in the garden. In the summer months, my sister and brother-in-law take them for a swim in the river. There is something paradisiacal about this place.

As we pass by the geese and walk down the dirt path, we come upon our family well. It's been there ever since I can remember. We water our garden with the well water. In the summer months we drink from it to quench our thirst. And just beyond the well is a bench carefully positioned by a fishpond. In the summer months, many frogs populate the pond, croaking away to their hearts' desire.

> *We are thirsty for a great abundance.*

We don't often sit on that bench by the well.

We are a busy family, and sitting still is not something that comes easily. Working hard is probably the most venerated virtue in our family. *Why do we push ourselves so hard?* I often wonder. What is it in me that doesn't give me permission to sit still and pause and take in the wonders that are all around me? It's hard because when I calm down and sit still, all that I am afraid of comes and haunts me. It seems easier to push these fears away and let them grind away in the deep crevices within.

It's terrifying to listen to the deeper and more painful things that haunt us from within. We often don't even have the language anymore to give names to the turmoil we feel inside. It's too easy to ignore it and lock away those feelings we don't like. Perhaps we have become so used to not feeling and have become numb to it. Anxiety and anger—or worse, fear and hate, shame and sadness, loneliness and despair—merge into one gray fog and leave us groping in the dark. It seems easier just to keep on coping.

We learn early to anesthetize ourselves. Many use work to anesthetize themselves and numb the pain within. Others go shopping or comfort eat, and others still use alcohol. I am thirsty. We all are thirsty.

THIRSTING FOR MORE

But reconnecting with and quenching emotional and spiritual thirst is no simple matter. It calls us to become pilgrims to waters that will quench our deepest thirst. It demands trust, courage, and time. Tapping into that living water is called prayer.

One of the stories in the Bible I've always loved is the story of Jesus at Jacob's well in the Gospel of John. Jesus and his disciples had a long day's journey on foot behind them. He was worn out, tired, and thirsty when they finally arrived at Sychar in Samaria. They stopped at the well just outside of the city, a well that had once belonged to their ancestor Jacob. The disciples left Jesus behind and went looking for food in the city.

And then something strange and radical happens. A Samaritan woman comes to the well. Samaritans were religious outcasts at that time, but this woman was also a social outcast, and Jesus knew it.

He could have gotten himself some water, but instead he says to the Samaritan woman, "Give me a drink."

We don't know much about the woman other than that she had lived a promiscuous life. Jesus doesn't seem to care. He neither judges nor avoids the woman as his culture expected him to do. Didn't he know the filth of that woman would make him unclean? What was he thinking? He doesn't seem to care. Instead, he asks her for a cup of water. If you want to translate his request "Give me a drink" into our time, it means that he covered her shame. He lifted her out of the mire into the dignity of a human being. It doesn't seem like much to us, but back then it was a radical gesture of welcome and acceptance.

> "Nature would certainly be satisfied with water to drink; and therefore the addition of wine is owning to God's superabundant liberality."
>
> JOHN CALVIN (1509–1564), FRENCHMAN AND REFORMER

His radical embrace of that woman—we never learn her name—opens up a conversation between them. And only then does Jesus confront the woman with her deeper thirst and poverty. He cuts right through to the core of things and offers her what she really needs: living water that quenches and soothes the poorest, most wretched and vulnerable part of her being. He names a thirst that the woman perhaps didn't even realize she had. Maybe she had given up on ever finding what she really needed. Maybe she had accepted her lot as a religious and social outcast, as the filth of the earth, and stopped longing for more. We don't know. But Jesus offers her living water, and hope begins to arise within her, hope for healing and forgiveness, hope for acceptance and true belonging. It really is a beautiful story full of love, compassion, and hope.

What has always struck me most about this story is that Jesus doesn't begin by confronting the woman. He doesn't say to the woman, "Your sins are forgiven." Instead, he invites her to open her eyes to the gifts of God. He instills a longing within her for a great abundance of living waters, a wellspring that will never run dry and will quench her deepest thirst.

Pause for a moment and take that in. Jesus' disarming embrace of her allows her to dare to hope. She finds herself loved and embraced by someone who does not judge her or intensify her shame. He knows, welcomes, and loves her in ways she perhaps has never known before.

The woman at the well lived in a culture that punished her for the sins she committed. They made her an outcast and withheld the most fundamental gift humans can give to one another: community. Our natural tendency is to punish one another for the shortcomings we face in ourselves and others. Jesus breaks this cycle and reveals God's radical love and forgiveness for those who are thirsty and willing to drink.

It's a story I return to over and over again. It reminds me of how hard it often is to get in touch and stay in touch with our emotional and spiritual thirst. Perhaps this is so because we don't find many places of radical love and forgiveness. Where are those places and who are the people we can entrust our vulnerable lives to and find a haven where we can safely unfold our brokenness and await the healing that we yearn for? I certainly haven't found them easily, and it often takes a lot of hard work to find them.

When we don't have those safe havens in our lives, it's easy to neglect that part of our lives or pretend it doesn't exist. Our comforts drawn from physical realities, such as water and wine or food and sex, are important, but they can only get us so far. They are just as integral to our spiritual lives as other gifts, but it's easy to get stuck in the physicality of them. Like all gifts, they are supposed to open our lives to the One they emanate from. God is the source of all good things, but when we aren't able to connect with God and one another through them, then we have lost touch. We get stuck like the woman at the well.

> *"Wine is like rain: when it falls on the mire it but makes it the fouler, But when it strikes the good soil wakes it to beauty and bloom."*
> JOHN HAY (1838–1905), AMERICAN POET

Our emotional and spiritual needs are harder to identify; perhaps they are hidden in more elusive and mysterious places of our lives. It takes more effort and wisdom to understand them and a loving community to uphold us as we journey with them. When Jesus challenges the woman to step out of her role as an outcast, she rediscovers herself as a creature of God and finally meets the One she really belongs to. In Jesus she finds abundant generosity of love and kindness, acceptance and mercy. We yearn for more. We yearn for something deeper, fuller, more lasting and enduring. We yearn for unconditional love, forgiveness, and acceptance. We yearn for a cup flowing over with the abundance of life.

THE WEDDING FEAST OF CANA

The other story from John's Gospel my family always returns to is the wedding feast of Cana. This story connects so well with our wine world. I guess we feel at home in it. It is the story about Jesus' first miracle of turning water into wine at a Jewish peasant wedding feast to teach people about the kingdom of heaven. What's so remarkable about this story is that Jesus doesn't just transform water into wine, he transforms a huge amount of water into an abundance of choice wine. The six big stone jars of water that Jesus transformed into wine contained somewhere between 480 and 720 liters; that would be between 640 and 960 bottles of wine today. Can you imagine that much wine at a wedding? And this wine was not run-of-the-mill, cheap supermarket wine. It was high-quality wine. It would have been worth a great deal of money. I've seen a lot of feasts and celebrations growing up in the wine world but never on such a grand scale.

The wine was so delicious that the responsible sommelier at the wedding was completely astonished by its beauty and quality, so much so that he interrupts the celebration and turns to the groom in wonder: "Everyone serves the good wine first, and then the inferior wine after the guests have become drunk. But you have kept the good wine until now" (John 2:10). Yes, you have read correctly. The wedding guests weren't only jolly and tipsy and intoxicated; they couldn't even appreciate the choice, delicious, and expensive wine anymore. *What a waste*, one could be tempted into thinking, but are generosity and beauty really a waste?

ABUNDANCE AND JOY

What is so moving about this wedding feast of Cana is that Jesus isn't satisfied with just quenching our thirst with water to help us survive in this world. He provides abundant wine to help us cultivate a festive spirit and learn to flourish together. He wants to give us a glimpse into what this life on earth is meant to be and draw us into the great love affair between God and his people.

He wants to show us that this life is not merely about survival but about blossoming into a love affair beyond compare. Christ as the bridegroom welcomes and embraces his beloved bride, the church. The abundance of wine hints at the abundance of love, grace, and faithful devotion that we find in Jesus Christ.

The abundance of wine also provides the raw and physical material to help the guests enter into this reality as they celebrate with feasting and dancing, singing and merry-making. Jesus enters the celebrations of ordinary and probably quite poor peasant people. He joins right in the hustle and bustle, the singing and dancing, the eating and drinking. He shares their joy and then expands and broadens and prolongs their experience of physical pleasure and the joy that comes from such sensual delights so their eyes might be opened to greater things yet to come.

I think a lot of us still have a hard time envisioning Jesus as someone who wants to intensify our experience of earthly pleasures. But that's what this story is about—at least in part. Perhaps bringing pleasure and joy was just as important, or perhaps even more important, to Jesus' ministry as feeding the poor or healing the sick. Joy is scarce and hard to come by in our time, and yet it lies at the heart of Jesus' ministry. Weddings are joyous occasions, and Jesus had no quibbles about joining in. He didn't think it was a waste of time.

But it all nearly went awry. The hosts had run out of wine and were about to expose themselves to great embarrassment and shame. You just don't run out of wine at a wedding feast. Why they didn't stock up on their wines, we don't know, but probably because they were poor. We do know that the servants couldn't refill the wine cups because there was no more wine. How awkward! Empty cups at a wedding celebration? Would the guests start complaining or quietly pass over this hugely embarrassing situation? The whole party could have come to a halt.

> *"No wine can be regarded as unimportant, my friend, since the marriage at Cana."*
>
> **GRAHAM GREENE (1904–1991), ENGLISH NOVELIST**

But no. Jesus steps in and saves the day. He miracles forth such an abundance of fantastic wine that the celebrations extend to unforeseen culinary delights. Fragrant, aromatic, and delicious wine flows into the empty wine cups. Jesus transforms scarcity into abundance, barrenness into intoxicating fruit. The wedding feast could have become a disaster, but instead Jesus transformed a humble peasant wedding feast into a royal banquet.

Most of the wedding guests probably didn't even notice. But some did and were astonished. Savor this thought for a while. Through this extravagant miracle, Jesus reveals to us something about God's nature, the very core of who he is. It's as if Jesus wants to open our eyes to God's abundant, beautiful, and life-giving presence among us. When you are surrounded by hardship and poverty, suffering and oppression, as they were in Jesus' time, that's difficult to believe.

God's economy seems a bit different from ours. He is generous beyond measure and doesn't seem to mind if some of his lavish gifts go unnoticed or seem wasted. I think it's hard to capture his great generosity in words. Miracles will have to do. Through this first miracle of turning water into wine, Christ revealed his glory. What are we to make of this miraculous gift of an abundance of fantastic wine that reveals God's glory?

Wine is to move us to a place of wonder, astonishment, and awe. Wine is to create a space for us, to open our eyes to God's grandeur and splendor, his majesty and beauty, his life-giving presence among us. Wine is to help us connect with God and open our eyes to new horizons, to the sacred that is right here with us. Wine is to re-enchant the world for us and help us see it anew—ablaze with God's glory.

CHAPTER FOUR

WINE IS GOD'S WAY
OF KISSING HUMANITY

He brought me to his wine cellar and his banner over me is love.

Song of Songs 2:4 (author's translation)

few years back I interviewed about thirty vintners from different countries about the spiritual dimension of wine. One of the most memorable conversations I had was with a vintner from Santa Barbara, California. Jo hadn't grown up with wine and only discovered it in college. He had taken on a job in a wine shop and gotten to know some of his customers quite well. One day a customer brought him a special bottle of Pinot Noir wine from the Côte de Nuits region in Burgundy, France. It was a 1978 Clos de la

Roche Grand Cru (the name of the vineyard) from Domaine Dujac (the name of the winery). Burgundy is an important place for what many today would consider great wine.

Many Burgundian vintners work hard to let a particular parcel of land—like Clos de la Roche—sing its earthy and haunting song through the wines it produces. For many wine lovers Burgundy has become the "promised land" of wine because the beauty is not just in the wine but also in the way the wine reflects a particular place. Some of those wine lovers have made it a life goal to visit that sacred place—first hallowed by Benedictine and Cistercian monks. They want to walk in its vineyards, smell the soil, breathe in the air, and feel the presence there. It's like a homecoming to them. They feel a special connection to that particular place on earth because of the ethereal wine that they have been able to savor. In a world where many wonder what home actually means, feeling a connection with a particular place is something very special—even more so when it's rich in history and laden with beauty.

> *"To treat a poor wretch with a bottle of Burgundy . . . is like giving a pair of laced ruffles to a man that has never a shirt on his back."*
>
> TOM BROWN
> (1663–1704),
> ENGLISH POET
> AND SATIRIST

Jo kept that precious bottle for just the right moment. He vividly remembers uncorking that bottle and how the most wonderful aromas slowly wafted out of the glass like smoke from dry ice. The smell or bouquet of the wine was intense and heavy and absolutely beautiful. Jo was enchanted. When he finally tasted the wine, he felt he was going to levitate off the ground. He had never in his life tasted anything so beautiful and delicious. It was as if he had been transported into another place, a place of beauty, passion, and mystery. He felt awe, wonder, and astonishment.

That moment changed his life. He had a conversion experience right then and decided to become a vintner. Jo set out on a life's journey to re-create such beautiful wines in his own native Southern California. He set out to learn from those who had gone before to craft wines that would reflect the natural places where the vines grew. He wanted to reenchant the world with the wonders and delights of wine and share his own epiphany with his fellow Americans.

Where I come from we have a saying that wine is God's way of kissing humanity. I think that is what happened to Jo. There can be something so delicious, enlivening, and enchanting about savoring a glass of good wine that it delights and lifts the human spirit to unimagined places and, yes, encounters.

Savoring a beautiful wine is about encounter—not just with the wine but also with the place where it comes from, the soil where the vines flourish,

> *"The boy once more filled the glasses. This time the Brothers and Sisters knew that what they were given to drink was not wine, for it sparkled. It must be some kind of lemonade. The lemonade agreed with their exalted state of mind and seemed to lift them off the ground, into a higher and purer sphere."*
>
> ISAK DINESEN (1885–1962), AUTHOR OF *BABETTE'S FEAST*

the climate and the loving hand of the vintner. In a time when many of us feel detached from the places where we live, a wine that reflects place invites us to connect with those places and come to love those places, perhaps for the first time. It makes us feel more at home in this world. It can open our hearts to those we share the wine with and ultimately to the Giver of all good gifts. Savoring wine is about coming home. It's God's way of wooing us back to see heaven coming down to earth and lifting us up to a place of wonder.

HE BROUGHT ME TO HIS WINE CELLAR

The Song of Songs is all about this sense of wonder and astonishment and how wine, just like erotic love, can elevate our spirits to moments of intense pleasures and where earthly and heavenly joys meet and mingle. This beautiful and sensual love poem was very popular in medieval times. Respected theologians understood it to be about Christ, the bridegroom, and the church, his bride. They probably did so because it recalls the imagery of the Garden of Eden.

Bernard of Clairvaux from Burgundy was one of those theologians. This Burgundian monk and mystic placed divine love at the center of all things. It was his favorite spiritual theme, and he never tired of it. The Song of Songs became a great fount of inspiration for him as he explored this mystical love affair between Christ and his bride. Bernard was a great charismatic figure who soon had countless followers. They came from far and near and left their old lives behind in order to follow Bernard into this great love affair.

However, Bernard's attention to the Song of Songs did something quite unexpected to these monks, something that theologians to this day neglect to speak about, perhaps because they think it is not spiritual enough. The Song of Songs helped inspire Bernard's fellow monks to plant those now famous Grand Cru vineyards in Burgundy. These monks began to perfect the growth of Pinot Noir in Burgundy. Their devotion to God fermented into devotion to the land and to crafting wine of superior quality. What else could reflect this great love but choice wine served in the Lord's Supper, the most intimate place where the beloved would meet? Wine became part of this great love affair just like the Song of Songs expressed it. Crafting beautiful wine was one way for the monks to demonstrate their love of God and bring glory to his name. It became an act of worship.

Over time, these Burgundian wines became renowned throughout the Holy Roman Empire, and kings and noblemen sought out these wines because of their great beauty. Today, Burgundy has become once more one of the most renowned wine regions of the world. When wine lovers flock to Burgundy to pay homage to the vineyards of Romanée-Conti, Clos de Vougeot, and Clos de la Roche, few remember how and why they came into being. They still hint at the great love affair these monks once had, a love affair grounded in the earth where the vineyards, under the loving hands of devoted monks, came to voice praise to their Creator.

> *"The chef, surprisingly enough, was a woman . . . . This woman . . . had the ability to transform a dinner into a kind of love affair, a love affair that made no distinction between bodily appetite and spiritual appetite."*
>
> ISAK DINESEN (1855–1962),
> AUTHOR OF *BABETTE'S FEAST*

Even today the Song of Songs wants to draw us into the drama, tension, and beauty of two lovers and their intimate yearning and musings. It's not just a poem about the love between God and his people but also about the love that two lovers share and delight in. Sadly, for many of us, this poem has remained a closed book. There is no apparent moral to this poem, and perhaps this explains why we haven't used it much in modern times; we just don't know what to do with it. It's a bit unsettling to the moral compass and to eager pilgrims who rigorously and obediently seek to align their will to the will of God, to those who feel uncomfortable with enjoying earthly pleasures as a way to see the kingdom of God come down to earth.

Perhaps it is time to overcome our inhibitions and allow ourselves to enter and be moved, delighted, and transformed by the love poetry of this beautiful book of the Bible. The rich poetry, together with the enjoyment of some well-crafted wine, will help you relax, enjoy, and celebrate these special moments as we take delight in them and experience pleasure from them.

"Let him kiss me with the kisses of his mouth! / For your love is better than wine" (Song of Songs 1:2), writes the poet. The sensual experience of touching wine with your lips, the tingling sensation of the alcohol on your tongue and in your throat, and the delicious aromas of the wine can enchant and delight and, yes, slightly intoxicate you. Allow yourself to open up to the spiritual experience that it was meant to be. Each beckons the other. Deep calls unto deep. What can be better than wine? The true love between two devoted lovers, the bride and the groom, who anticipate and desire and yearn for nuptial delight and bliss. Come, Lord Jesus, come.

AND HIS BANNER OVER US IS LOVE

To grasp the love of God for this world has always been one of the most difficult spiritual pilgrimages. Too many other paths keep us traveling below our highest calling; too many other voices drown out that gentle and most intimate whisper of God's love. The Song of Songs and the first of Jesus' miracles at the wedding of Cana insist we cannot reduce the Christian faith to a set of rules to follow, idealized virtues to measure up to, and a moral compass that keeps us in check on the narrow path of sacrificial living.

The Song of Songs, just like the miracle of Cana, has always carried another dimension of meaning. It resonates back to the Garden of Eden. The Hebrew word for *Eden* literally means enjoyment and delight. The ideal spiritual state in the biblical vision is that God and his people live in harmony and peace in a garden of great beauty with an abundance of delicious food. Together they enjoy the pure bliss of mutual love and innocent delight in the fruits of the earth, and, yes, that includes wine.

In the book that follows right after the Song of Songs, the prophet Isaiah envisions God as the bridegroom and his people as his bride. Isaiah believed God's redemption will be like a great feast with choice wine for all people. The prophet Hosea even compares God's redemption to a grand wedding banquet in which all living creatures participate.

Then in the New Testament, when Jesus transformed water into an abundance of fantastic wine—and saved the groom from potential humiliation—he stepped into the role of the bridegroom and took the wedding guests to another party altogether. Through this miracle Jesus gave us a vision of a greater feast yet to come, a heavenly wedding banquet where the wine of salvation will flow to all who are willing to join the feast. The prophets had hinted at it, but in Jesus this feast has actually begun. Yes, a real feast with real food and real wine, lively music, and lots of dancing becomes a place of revelation.

Jesus reveals the glory of God when he makes sure there is such a great amount of wonderful wine to help the wedding guests celebrate into eternity. This miracle melts away the boundaries between heaven and earth, time and eternity, and invites us to join in.

> *What would Jesus drink? Wine, of course.*

What would Jesus drink? Wine, of course, to continue the heavenly wedding banquet that will resound throughout time and bids us to join in and come home.

CHAPTER FIVE

COMING HOME

*During Solomon's lifetime Judah and Israel lived in
safety, . . . all of them under their vines and fig trees.*

1 KINGS 4:25

$\mathcal{M}$y father has always made sure that I would have some family
wine no matter where I was. Whether I happened to live in
Canada, Holland, the United States, or Scotland, my family always
sent me a case of the family wine for Christmases and birthdays.

Whenever I open a bottle of our dry, fresh and crisp, and savory
Silvaner wine, it smells like home. It takes me right back to that place
where I grew up, and I feel that strong connection. It's not just a
connection with my people but also with our land, the soil and the

weather, our history and our faith. And wine unlocks that connection for me and throws me right back into the arms of my upbringing.

With all the moving and traveling I have done, times when I can share some of my favorite Kreglinger wine with friends around the dinner table have always helped me feel more settled and at home—no matter where I was. When I feel lost in the world—and yes, sometimes I do feel lost—a little glass of family wine cradles and comforts me. It connects me to where I come from and also creates a bond with those I now share life with. They learn a little bit more about who I am and where I come from, and it creates a longing in them to visit the place where I was born and raised. It brings us together, and each sip creates a bond of knowing and understanding that will always be beyond the grasp of language.

You don't have to grow up on a winery to have those feelings of connection through a well-crafted wine. The wine itself can create those bonds as it reflects and connects us with a particular place and time (vintage). Wine can take you to places you never thought you would know. A Chianti Classico will take you to Tuscany, a Pinot Gris might take you to the Alsace region in France, a Riesling to the Mosel region in Germany, a Pinot Noir to the Willamette Valley in Oregon, and Cabernet Sauvignon to Napa, California. Just start the journey yourself and look for wines that seek to reflect a particular place and region. You will be astounded to learn how particular and unique these wines are and how familiar they will become after you have enjoyed them repeatedly.

When you make beer or whiskey, it doesn't really matter where you grow grain for it. It's what you do with the grain that matters. With grapes it is very different.

HOW WINE REFLECTS PLACE

Where the grapes grow, the soil, the sun exposure, the rain, the wind and the stillness, the fog rolling over the hills from the rivers or the sea, and the hand of the vintner will all shape the taste of the wine and make each vintage sing its unique song. If you try a Pinot Noir from the Côte de Nuits in Burgundy and compare it to a Pinot Noir from the Willamette Valley in Oregon or Central Otago in New Zealand, you will find that they taste different from each other. Even without any previous wine knowledge, you would be able to taste the differences and be amazed!

Well-crafted wines have a way of wedding us to the earth that is rather unique. Perhaps they create a stirring in us, a stirring to feel more connected and to be more at home in this world.

I've always wondered whether this connection, this sense of home, is what some of our customers are searching for when they come to visit the winery and linger there for a while. They want to know about the place, the soil, the weather and how that's reflected in the wine. It's usually the people from the city who ask, people who have lost their connection with the land. It feels as if they are searching for that connection and somehow and somewhere want to find it again and take it back to the city.

> *"And that you may the less marvel at my words, Look at the sun's heat that becomes wine When combined with the juice that flows from the vine."*
>
> **DANTE ALIGHIERI (1265–1321), ITALIAN POET AND THEOLOGIAN**

Our human desire to belong and connect not only with people but also with place, and especially natural places, is perhaps one of the greatest longings of our time. The most immediate and also most intimate way we connect with place is through what we eat and drink. But most of that connection has been lost. People used to have a much closer connection to the land as they grew their own fruit and veggies. They used to know the local miller and baker, the cattle farmer and butcher, the local fishermen and fishmonger, and local farmers who grew fruit and veggies for their community. Part of shopping was connecting with those people, their work, and their products, and through them with the land. It was one interconnected community with all the joys and challenges that such a community brings.

Most of this has gone. Corporations have taken over the work of small family-owned businesses, and multinational corporations process the food that we now eat. Supermarkets perpetuate that impersonal and disconnected way of shopping, eating, and drinking. We've lost something that we didn't even realize we needed, a connection to place. Home is a more complex reality than we think. It's not only about people but also about place and the seasons and the soil and the fruit of the earth.

> *We've lost something that we didn't even realize we needed, a connection to place.*

Why small family-owned wineries have been able to survive the onslaught of big corporations and industrial food processing is still a puzzle to me. How long will it last?

Our local baker closed down decades ago and our local butcher only a few years ago, but family-owned wineries are still a regular feature of village life, and you can find them all over Europe. It's harder for them now because they have to compete with big corporations, but they have survived because they have something special and important to give. Perhaps their work is prophetic for our time. When so few of us are connected to the earth, they can help us rediscover that the earth and what it brings forth is our home. Without it we would be no more.

THE VINTNERS THAT MAKE US FEEL AT HOME

When vintners set out to craft wine that reflects place, they offer us not just something profoundly beautiful but also profoundly meaningful. As the wine mirrors a natural place, it invites us into a great mystery—a living organism, a dynamic dance of place, work, and play that is full of vitality and presence. As we learn to savor this mysterious world, we will get glimpses of reality that can evoke astonishment. It's both a gift of nature and the product of dedicated and careful craftsmanship. For vintners to craft such beautiful wine, they have to make themselves at home in the vineyard and come to know it intimately. Only through this kind of knowing, carried by devoted love and care, are they able to let the vineyard sing its enchanting song.

> *"Back of this wine is the vintner, And back through the years his skill, And back of it all are the vines in the sun And the rain and the Master's Will."*
>
> VINTNER'S ODE

And yet for us consumers it is so easy to forget how amazing it is that wine exists at all. It's so easy to get accustomed to great wonders and cease to be in awe. For some of us it's tempting to dismiss it all as unimportant, especially those of us who are spiritually inclined. Isn't our real home in heaven? Why should we bother feeling more connected here on earth? Aren't we too earthbound anyway?

Being and feeling connected to the earth is one of the most urgent endeavors of our time. Through wholesome connection comes love, and through love comes care. We need the earth, and the earth needs our love and care. The ability of wine to mirror natural places can give us that sense of connection to particular places, teach us to love those places, and give us the courage to care for them.

Wine invites us to come home, to make ourselves more at home in this world and realize that we belong to this amazing and deeply interconnected community.

You don't have to live on a winery or come from a winery or a wine region to be able to experience this sense of connection and homecoming with and through wine. As you discover wines you enjoy and familiarize yourself with the wine and where it comes from, you can share the wine and your passion for it with others. When you go to a wine tasting, a winery, or a wine shop, or have dinner some place and discover a wine you love, take a couple of those bottles home or take a picture of the label so you can track it down later.

Invite some friends to dinner or even just for wine and nibbles. As you gather around the table and introduce your friends to this newly discovered wine, share the story of how you discovered the wine and why you like it. There is something beautiful about sharing the wines we love with others and this sense of delight and homecoming we feel as we enjoy it. It's a lovely way to share life with one another as we savor and enjoy the fruits of creation and through it feel more connected to the earth itself.

I love Rieslings from the Rheingau in Germany, and their floral and fruity fragrance continues to delight and surprise me. It is always such a joy when I can share a well-crafted and delicate Riesling with friends who might never gravitate to a Riesling wine. More often than not my friends suddenly find themselves surprised and enchanted, feeling a bit more at home in this world that can bring forth such bountiful and intricate flavors in just one small glass of wine.

CHAPTER SIX

MAKING PEACE WITH WINE AND FOOD

To drink is to pray, to binge-drink is to sin.

GERMAN PROVERB

As beautiful as wine and food can be, for many of us our relationship with wine and food is wrought with tension. We live in a fast-paced world where eating and drinking are often reduced to fueling our bodies. Many of us are busy, mostly behind schedule, and working hard to keep it all together. Who has the luxury of pausing, pondering, and enjoying the beauty of a fine wine and a carefully prepared meal?

At mealtimes I often find myself wolfing down my food, thinking of all the things I still need to do. When I do have a glass of wine with my meal, which does not happen every day, I have to remind myself over and over to savor the wine and not gulp it down. Alas, it often happens that when I lift up my eyes from the plate and look around the table, I find that my plate and my wine glass are empty before anyone else's.

I don't eat and drink too much; I just eat and drink too fast.

I hate that I do this and admire those who have mastered the art of eating and drinking slowly—those who even in the midst of a hectic life seem to be able to switch off, slow down, and be present and savor. I find it difficult.

THE BATTLEGROUND OF EATING AND DRINKING

Eating and drinking are some of the most fundamental things we do as human beings on a daily basis. They are supposed to be enjoyable and comforting and bring nourishment and healing to our bodies, minds, and spirits. When we turn eating and drinking into a spiritual practice, a ritual, it can feed our bodies and our souls. Eating and drinking traditionally connected us with one another as we shared a meal around the table, to the earth from which our foods come, and ultimately with God, the Giver of all good things. The bounty of the earth is a continual reminder that God has not abandoned this world. He is benevolent toward us in ways we might never fully grasp.

Karen MacNeil in *The Wine Bible* wrote that wine and food cradle us in our own communal humanity. That is a beautiful way of putting it.

The only problem is that for many people eating and drinking have become battlegrounds often hidden in secrecy. Let's face it—food is a great way to comfort oneself. And if you have grown up in a family with a pattern of overeating, it's difficult to break that pattern. It's a daily struggle and a vicious cycle. When not enough other comforts are around, it's easy to indulge in food. Perhaps you don't even know how to comfort yourself in ways that nourish you and feed the deep places within, not just physically but emotionally and spiritually. Perhaps our culture has forgotten how to create those places, times, and rituals that feed and comfort and cradle us in our naked and vulnerable humanity.

Eating and drinking disorders abound today, with some eating too little and others eating and drinking too much, mostly of the wrong sort of food and drink. Especially for women, food and drink have become battlegrounds. The media has manipulated women, men, and children into believing that women have to be skinny, tall, without natural blemishes, and sexy in order to be beautiful. These powerful and consistent visual messages infiltrate girls at a young age and subtly suggest to us girls and women that we are not enough. We look at our bodies and quickly realize we don't measure up. It's a subtle process, but it's real and affects us more than we are ready to admit. The media feeds on the insecurities of women and adjusts their marketing accordingly to make and keep us feeling inadequate. It's a lucrative business because we are willing to spend a lot of money trying to fix the "problem."

> *"In water one sees
> one's own face:
> But in wine
> one beholds the
> heart of another."*
> FRENCH PROVERB

How did this happen? Have we forgotten all those medieval and early modern paintings that celebrate the natural and well-rounded curves of women? Voluptuous beauty doesn't exist for the media, and we have silently consented to this disturbing and ever-so-subtle propaganda. We don't even question it anymore. It has made many women hate their bodies. Without even noticing it, eating and drinking have become battlegrounds for them. Calories have become enemies. Too many women can no longer savor and enjoy their food and wine because of this propaganda. They see these gifts as a threat to their body shape.

It's difficult not to internalize the constant bombardments of utopian images of women's bodies. It's very subtle; the marketing world has done its work well and we must learn to resist it and learn to celebrate our curves, folds, and wrinkles. We need to learn to be free to nurture all of our senses and savor those moments of delight when they come. They give us glimpses into the very heart of what it means to be alive and celebrate life for the gift it is. Life is not about incessantly trying to measure up to a utopian ideal we can never reach. There is no grace and no joy in that.

In addition to a wide range of eating disorders, an increasing number of people have allergic reactions to a wide range of foods and don't quite know how to feed themselves. The nutritional value of food and drink in the Western world has gone down for decades. We have a seeming abundance of food and drink in the West, more than we've ever had, but how nourishing is it? Much of the foods offered in the supermarkets are actually making us sick. Eating has become a complex and painful reality for many, and there is no end in sight to this widespread disease.

Still others struggle with alcohol abuse, and many have alcohol abuse in their family histories. Their relationship with alcohol has remained ambivalent to say the least. To enjoy wine well takes wisdom. As with all good things, wine can be abused, and we must cultivate and model a healthy and wholesome engagement with wine. Those who struggle with alcohol addiction might have to abstain from wine altogether.

Most people, however, have to learn how to drink wine in life-giving ways. I do not believe that the answer to overindulgence and alcohol abuse is merely temperance. It's part of our response, but I believe there is more we can do to cultivate a healthy relationship with wine. As we learn to savor wine with greater mindfulness, we allow ourselves to grow in our awareness that we need to feed more than our bodies. Rather than just trying to tame our impulse to gulp down wine (or wolf down food), we can learn to channel this impulse toward a greater attentiveness and appreciation of what we consume.

> "Wine in moderation—not in excess, for that makes men ugly—has a thousand pleasant influences. It brightens the eye, improves the voice, imparts a new vivacity to one's thoughts and conversation."
>
> CHARLES DICKENS
> (1812–1870),
> ENGLISH NOVELIST

Drinking wine, like eating food, is to bring nourishment to our bodies and our souls. Wine enjoyed in moderation and shared around the dinner table can and should help forge alliances of peace in our families, local communities, and even beyond the bounds of our countries.

A couple years back I was in contact with a lawyer from the United States, and we corresponded back and forth about wine and its impact on our lives. I was deeply moved by his reflection on how wine has played an important role in international affairs between the United States and other countries:

> Last evening I was at a graduation ceremony for 39 international students from about 25 countries who were in the United States as part of an exchange program for allied military officers. We had a wonderful reception, good wine and food; and as usual, relationships between international officers develop with their US counterparts in this casual and celebratory setting. I know of several times when these relationships have defused serious incidents between the US and other countries because of the common bond developed over meals.

This wonderful reflection has stayed with me, and such an account should not surprise us but inspire us. The rejection of wine on a grand scale just because of the fear of alcohol abuse is not the answer. All things can and will be abused, but wine enjoyed with wisdom can enrich our lives in the most unexpected ways. The bonds forged over wine and food can have ripple effects far beyond our wildest dreams.

It's so important to keep such memories alive because for many families dinner together around the table has all but disappeared from their daily lives. Some children don't even know anymore what a dinner table is. Life is just too busy and hectic. It's easier to grab food on the way.

Perhaps it is better to say that wine and food used to cradle us in our own communal humanity. Those days might be long gone for you, or they may have never been a reality for you at all.

COMFORT AND SAFETY

Many of us have to relearn what it means to develop a nurturing environment for ourselves in which we feel safe, loved, and comforted, where food and wine can help us feel cradled in our communal humanity once more and where we don't feel imprisoned and enslaved by it.

My family has developed some important rules and rhythms for drinking wine to ensure that we don't abuse it. With easy access to an abundance of wine in the cellar, we have to make sure we don't abuse wine to cope with the stress and pain of our lives. Those who make their living by crafting and selling wine can't afford to get into trouble with alcohol abuse.

Over many generations we have learned to cultivate a healthy relationship with wine. We don't usually drink wine before five p.m. except on Sundays, and we only have a couple of glasses with our meal shared around the dinner table. Wine is meant to be shared. It's a communal experience for us. We don't drink wine every day to make sure we don't become dependent on it.

My family also has a small distillery on the winery, and we craft strong spirits such as brandy distilled from our wine and schnapps from the pears, plums, and apples that grow on the fruit trees of our orchard. We are even more careful with these strong distilled spirits, and we don't drink them on a regular basis. They are treats for special occasions enjoyed under the scrutiny of a watchful community.

There are exceptions to all these guidelines, such as important family celebrations like birthdays, baptisms, confirmations, weddings, and big anniversaries. Then wine flows more freely, and the celebrations often last well into the night with lots of long conversations, laughter, dancing, and merrymaking. Only in looking back do I realize how much these celebrations have fed our communal spirits and made me feel less lonely and vulnerable in this increasingly fractured world we live in.

Growing up, our weak, tender, and most vulnerable spots were overeating and working too much. And it is probably there that my own battles with food emerged. We devote much care to growing food, preparing meals, and enjoying them, but looking back I realize that we sought too much comfort in food.

Grandma was a fantastic cook and always made sure there was plenty of delicious food on the table. It was amazing to watch what feasts Grandma could conjure up in her very humble kitchen. My grandfather was always a more-than-enthusiastic recipient. He lived to eat.

Oma's cozy kitchen was a special place to me. It was *her* space, and we were wise not to meddle with her in that kitchen. With priestly devotion she worked tirelessly to satisfy our appetites. Her kitchen became my sanctuary, and that's where I learned about the sacredness of food and drink. My dad inherited my grandparents' passion for food and wine, and the dinner table became the orbit around which our lives on the winery revolved.

WHERE DOES MY HELP COME FROM?

While we spent lots of time around the family table, it wasn't always the most emotionally nurturing of places. We tended to eat hastily, and the stress and tension of running a winery often hovered over us like a heavy fog. Dad always listened to the weather forecast to see what kind of work could be done in the vineyards, and Mom had to keep us four lively and sometimes wild girls in check lest my father's anger would flare up. They weren't the most comforting and soothing of times, those daily times around the table.

My parents were born during the trauma of the Second World War and grew up in its aftermath. A whole generation took on the survivor mentality to which children of the war tend to escape in order to cope with the trauma. My grandparents and parents found solace in rebuilding the ruins and working hard. It wasn't fashionable then to see a psychologist and work through the trauma, and they did not have the resources for it. They just learned to cope and "get on" with life. All that emotional stuff was downplayed, suppressed, and ignored.

I remember vividly the time when I had to decide how I would comfort myself. It was quite subconscious at first, but watching my family's love affair with food created an open invitation to overindulge and comfort myself this way.

As a teenager, I loved pasta. It is soft and soothing in the mouth and glides down the throat like a long and gentle hug, especially when smothered in the delicious tomato sauce my mom always made.

We always had a good supply of chocolate in the house, and German chocolate is delicious. I loved milk chocolate with grated and roasted coconut flakes in it. It felt creamy and smooth as it melted on my tongue, and its deep, rich flavor felt like a warm mantle that soothed the cold, anxious, and lonely feelings inside.

Food can provide that comfort, but it doesn't last very long, and then I'd have to eat again. It's like throwing myself into a dark abyss. It doesn't lead anywhere. It remains a vicious cycle.

SENSING SALVATION AND HEALING

For many teenagers a lifelong battle with eating and drinking disorders begins in those years between childhood and adulthood when we try to find our own place in this world. One of the times of my life I remember vividly as a young teenager was during preparation for my confirmation into the Lutheran faith. I was about to turn fourteen. Confirmations are a big deal in my family and the Lutheran culture. It was going to be a huge day, with relatives from near and far coming to witness this important step on my spiritual journey. It seemed that everyone from the village brought me cards and a little gift. Even some of my father's vintner colleagues and their families came to congratulate me. It was one of those days when my family celebrated well into the night with lots of wonderful food and fantastic wine.

I only remember feeling nervous. I begrudgingly put on my outfit, a hand-me-down from my sister, who is four years older than I am. My father did not see the point in buying me a new outfit when my older sister's fit so well. (It didn't make sense to him, and we needed all the money to keep the winery afloat.) *How could they expect me to wear such an old-fashioned outfit?* I thought. The strange frilly white collar of the blouse I wore beneath my black jacket had completely gone out of fashion. I felt embarrassed and ashamed as

I stood in line with my peers. To my great dismay, the only other girl in the group wore the trendiest and most fashionable outfit one could imagine, which only exacerbated my feelings of inferiority and being out of place.

Despite all of this teenage angst, something important happened to me on that day. During my confirmation into the Lutheran faith, I partook for the first time in my life in the Lord's Supper. I had learned a bit about this mysterious and wonderful ritual we call a sacrament. Now I realize that perhaps it really takes a lifetime to explore its meaning for our lives.

I had learned in my confirmation classes that as we partake in the Lord's Supper, as we eat from the one bread and drink wine from the one chalice, we receive the forgiveness of our sins. Somehow it had to do with Christ dying and being resurrected, but I really didn't understand how that was all connected and what that really meant. I think they were trying to say that God meant well with us. We had all memorized a little formula about it, stored it away in our overactive teenage brains, ready to recite it when called upon.

And then something unexpected happened. We youngsters all lined up in a neat row, nervously holding out our hands to receive the bread and opening our mouths to drink wine from the chalice. It was quiet and solemn. The whole church was packed and watched us closely.

When it was my turn to drink from the chalice and when the wine touched my lips, I was taken aback. I hadn't expected to smell and taste something so familiar. We were actually drinking my family's wine. The smell was so familiar, so fresh and crisp and strong, that it hurled me right back to our tasting room, to our winery and all the hustle and bustle that life on the winery brings.

It dawned on me then that perhaps this strange and mysterious ritual actually had something to do with our lives on the winery.

Perhaps God wasn't as far away as I had always thought him to be. I had a little revelation. Suddenly I realized that perhaps God cared. Perhaps God cared about our stressful lives on the winery and all the pain and sorrow that mingled too often with our joys and laughter.

It would take me decades to put into words what I had sensed at this moment of my confirmation, but it was like a doorway into an unknown world, a world of love and grace, of mercy and healing and forgiveness all experienced through a piece of bread and a sip of wine. I learned to draw on my sense of smell and taste to nurture my spiritual life. I began to sense salvation.

> *I learned to draw on my sense of smell and taste to nurture my spiritual life. I began to sense salvation.*

Now, over thirty years later, I continue to come back to this mysterious ritual where I taste the goodness of God in bread and wine. It is a place where I sense salvation and healing coming in such tangible ways like a sip of crisp and fresh and strong white wine or a sip of dark and sweet and rich red wine gliding down my throat like a warm blanket on a cold winter's day. It warms me from the inside out. It's soothing and tingles in my mouth and throat. It makes me feel more alive. It awakens the senses and alerts them to spiritual realities.

AMBIVALENT FEELINGS LINGER

Our senses are a gift from God, and through our senses we experience his goodness and that healing can come to us. Have you ever thought about the fact that two of the most important Christian practices, partaking in the sacraments of baptism and the Lord's Supper, invite us to sense salvation? We experience healing as sanctified water washes over us and as we chew bread from the one sanctified loaf and savor wine from the one sanctified cup. These sacraments call us to embrace and nurture our senses rather than keep them in check and deny their goodness.

We don't have to detach ourselves from food and wine in order to ascend to a higher spiritual realm. Instead, we learn to trust that God can redeem and heal our relationship with food and wine. We learn to lean into his healing presence. Now, people who struggle with addiction to alcohol have to be very careful, and they need to find their own unique way of recovery. They might have to stay away from alcohol for good. Those who struggle with food addiction or poor eating habits, on the other hand, can't just stay away from food. They have to find a path that allows them to develop a more wholesome relationship with it. It's tough, I am sure, but not eating is just not an option. Healing is the only path to wholeness.

The church hasn't always been helpful in all of this. There is still a deep ambivalence in many church communities regarding food and wine and certainly when it comes to understanding them as spiritual realities. At their best they will offer help to those who struggle with addiction, or they have a ministry to feed the poor. All of this is of course important, but there is so much more. How many churches embrace feasting as a spiritual practice and teach us to nurture our spiritual lives through food and wine, a feast for the senses? How can our relationship with food and wine be healed?

I believe we can take an important step toward healing our relationship with food and wine by understanding them as gifts from God. We can learn to see and cultivate eating and drinking as profoundly spiritual practices.

Traditionally, the church has taught us that the opposite of gluttony is temperance. There is truth to temperance, but it's only a half-truth. It leaves the best bit out of the equation. Temperance is about self-restraint, self-control, and moderation. It reacts to the danger of overindulgence. It reduces the gift of eating and drinking to a moral dilemma, or worse, a daily battleground. Those who suffer from eating disorders or alcohol abuse know how terrible, wearisome, and lonely this battle is. It's like a specter that haunts us wherever we go. It's like a deep dark hole that we can't crawl out of.

The temperance-gluttony paradigm assumes that the times of eating and drinking are first of all times of temptation rather than an invitation. And for too many of us it has become a self-fulfilling prophecy. Ambivalent feelings about food and wine as spiritual realities still linger, and it is time to overcome them.

CHAPTER SEVEN

TO DRINK IS TO PRAY

Attention in its highest form is prayer.

SIMONE WEIL

To receive wine as a gift from God means rediscovering the art of savoring as a form of prayer. It means becoming attentive to the subtle delights of food and wine and relishing their beauty. Gratitude for the gifts of God takes on the form of delight and prolonged pleasure as we learn to discover and recognize flavors and turn to joyful and grateful appreciation of them.

Growing up on a winery helped and taught me the art of paying attention to what I eat and drink. Our garden and tasting room on the winery have been sanctuaries for exploring with our lips, noses, and tongues the gifts of creation.

Our tasting room in particular is a purposefully created space where people get to slow down, attune their noses and tongues to the delights of the wines they taste, and then talk about what they sense in those wines. They get to reflect and enjoy and are permitted to express their delight or displeasure. They are allowed to savor and ponder the sensations they feel and indulge in them. It intensifies their enjoyment of the wines and can easily lift them out of the ordinary humdrum of daily life to a place of wonder.

> *"Come quickly, I am drinking stars!"*
>
> DOM PÉRIGNON (1638–1715), BENEDICTINE MONK, AFTER FIRST SAMPLING CHAMPAGNE

But most of life is not like that and most of us are continually pulled back into our frantic way of being in the world. Most places and spaces we inhabit don't create such moments of stillness and contemplation for us. On the contrary, for most of us our daily lives are shaped by relentless pressures and the need to hurry on to the next thing.

Even though I've grown up around a family that is intentional about savoring food and wine, I often find it difficult to slow down and be still. When I am on a mission, whether that's work, running errands, or cooking supper, my default mode is to focus, shift the inner engine to accomplish mode, and not get distracted on the way. I walk briskly just like my mom, and people often find it hard to keep up. It doesn't come naturally for me to find those precious moments of delight and wonder. It takes practice to make myself be still.

To enter into savoring as a form of prayer, we have to be intentional. It won't happen naturally because most of us have not been taught how to do this. We will have to go against the grain of our own intuitions, our culture, and even our church culture as we learn to cultivate a form of prayer that celebrates sensuous delights as a gift from God.

THE LIFE OF THE CHURCH AND SENSUAL DELIGHTS

What makes it even more difficult to embrace and cultivate savoring as a form of prayer is that smelling, touching, and tasting aren't sensations we value very much when it comes to the spiritual life and especially prayer. Most Protestant churches see very little use in our capacity to touch, smell, and taste. My Lutheran tradition is very heady, and I think quite unbalanced in the way we have cultivated the spiritual life. Words written, spoken, and sung define the way we do things, and these words have always left me hungry and thirsty for other ways of nurturing my spirituality.

When I began to realize that our senses of smell and taste can and should be called on as we cultivate the spiritual life, I suddenly was able to connect my faith much more with my daily life. There is so much beauty all around us, and we have to eat and drink daily, so why not use these opportunities to sense God's presence with us and notice the beauty he has placed into his creation for us to enjoy, savor, and share with one another?

This sensuous journey into the spiritual connectedness of heavenly and earthly realities also helped me realize that what we did on the winery—craft beautiful wine to bring joy to our customers— is a profoundly spiritual endeavor. Vintners attest to it all the time but they often don't find the words to express what they sense in growing vines, crafting wine, and sharing it with their customers. They sense they are involved in a profoundly spiritual undertaking, and yet they have not been given language to express it. They stand in awe but don't know where to direct their worship.

Embracing and training our God-given senses of smell and taste to enjoy the gifts of the earth is a spiritual path that we must rediscover. Its ultimate purpose is not merely to feed our bodies but also to help us reconnect with the earth and with God as the Giver of all good things. We were created to experience the Christian faith in fully embodied form, drawing on all of our senses to commune with the living God. As we ponder the Giver of these delectable gifts and learn to commune with the triune God in sensual delight, our lives will become more connected and integrated again. We will learn to saturate our daily lives with prayer.

DO THIS IN REMEMBRANCE OF ME

It was a fascinating journey of discovery for me when I learned from the neurosciences that the part of our brain that processes smells also processes emotions and memories. Somehow, smelling and tasting things stirs our feelings and helps us to remember.

It didn't take me long to make the connection to the Lord's Supper and how our sense of smell and taste helps us to ingest spiritual realities. When Jesus celebrated the Passover meal with his disciples and offered them bread and wine he said: "Do this in remembrance of me" (1 Corinthians 11:24). Feeding his disciples flavorful bread and fragrant wine is how Jesus taught his disciples. The thin, tasteless wafers we use today and the tiny sips of wine or grape juice don't do justice to the teaching that Jesus did through bread and wine.

In the celebration of the Passover meal—turned into the Lord's Supper—Jesus built on the tradition of his forefathers to cultivate his faith through feasts and celebrations. The sensual delights of a lamb roast, bitter herbs, bread, and wine helped his disciples ingest his teaching, connect it to the faith of their forefathers, and make it their own. It became a powerful place of revelation.

We have to rediscover how smelling and tasting fragrant wine in the Lord's Supper can help us ingest, remember, and celebrate God's truths and his healing presence in our midst. The act of remembering Christ's redemptive death on the cross can happen as much through our noses and tongues as it happens through seeing the bread broken and the cup raised and hearing the words spoken.

BAPTIZED NOSES AND TONGUES

Training our noses and tongues to sense salvation will be a journey as we learn to pay attention to smell and taste. We are so accustomed to focusing our attention on seeing, hearing, and talking that it is easy to hold a glass of wine in hand and never notice much of its flavor because we are so busy chatting, listening, and mingling. We have to train ourselves to pay attention to the sensations that register in our brains as smell and taste. It will take some practice. We need to nurture those neglected senses.

As we get into the habit of noticing them, it will be amazing to experience more and more of the smells and tastes around us and welcome them into our life. If you don't smell much when you first learn to taste wine, don't worry. It will come with time. As you sensitize yourself to those more subtle and unfamiliar smells, you will develop an alertness and the ability to notice and recognize them. Be patient with yourself. It just takes time.

I've been traveling all over the world to speak about the spirituality of wine and tasting wine as a spiritual practice. I try to create and hold a space for my guests in which they can discover and enjoy wine's spiritual blessings. At first people feel startled. They wouldn't naturally bring wine and faith together; nor would they see why savoring can and should become a form of prayer. I have to take them on a journey.

Many have never heard that wine is a gift from God that he gave quite specifically to make our hearts glad. They have to learn how savoring wine gladdens the human heart. At these events my presentations seamlessly flow over into a wine tasting. I want my guests to experience that they can take in teaching through what they hear and see *and* through what they smell and taste. I insist that all my events include a wine tasting so my guests can learn how to savor wine and allow it to nurture their souls and bring gladness to their hearts. Wine tastings can and should become a spiritual practice.

To drink is to pray.

SAVORING AND PILGRIM WAYS

In our Franconian wine culture we often say that to drink is to pray and to binge drink is to sin, and we all know that the line between praying and sinning can be a thin one indeed. Where is the line between enjoying a glass of wine, savoring it for its beauty, the fellowship and conviviality it creates, and abusing it, gulping it down to soothe one's anxieties and fears, to numb one's pain or ease one's boredom and loneliness? It takes wisdom to enjoy a glass of wine responsibly, patience to hear the song that a wine sings, and an open heart to follow its invitation to a more communal life. It demands our full attention, and that is difficult as we live in an age of constant distraction. But savoring is something we can and must learn because savoring wine in its highest form is prayer.

Learning to savor is like going on a pilgrimage. We don't learn to savor overnight. It takes time to learn to become more attentive to the delicate flavors in wine. As we learn to slow down and attune our senses to the gifts before us, we have to learn to become still, to calm all the noise and clutter inside and around us. It's like creating a little sanctuary in time so we can actually pay attention and nurture our senses.

Our physical thirst, just like our physical hunger, reminds us that we are always hungry and thirsty for more. Spiritual, emotional, and physical hunger and thirst naturally intermingle in our lives, and for some of us they come to the fore more forcefully when we eat and drink. Here, we can begin to pray and learn to understand ourselves a little more. Prayer gives us permission to allow our spiritual and emotional thirsts to find a voice in our lives. It's easy to neglect them.

Prayer gives us permission to allow our spiritual and emotional thirsts to find a voice in our lives.

This journey began for me when I awakened into adulthood and realized I had inherited my mom's intuitive way of coping with life: anxiety, fear, and worry. Mom never spoke of her fears and worries, but it's the nature of children to imbibe their parents' coping mechanisms, and for me it was my mom's propensity to open the door to anxiety and fear. Somehow, I intuited her lack of feeling safe in the world and made it my own. Learning to be still is a journey of letting go, shedding over time the things that shackle us and opening our senses to the wonders all around us.

This practice toward stillness has become a lifelong journey for me. When the deep places within pull me into the rut of anxiety and fear, I have to alert myself and choose to step out of this familiar treadmill. I have learned to embrace the wider space of hope that all will be well in the stillness of time. The joy of recognizing and celebrating the gifts all around me remind me of God's goodness and his generosity toward us. Savoring wine is one of those spiritual practices that creates a space where I get a glimpse into the heart of what it means to be alive. For a moment I can see and smell and taste and be moved by the wonder of all that earth brings forth in such concentrated form. I cease to be anxious and embrace gratitude and joy. Savoring wine invites us on a pilgrimage of wonder and delight.

SAVORING INTO WONDER

Savoring wine is like stepping into an orchard, a meadow, or a forest with our eyes and nose and tongue attuned to subtle delights. One of my favorite red wines is Pinot Noirs from Oregon. As I uncork the bottle and pour the wine into a glass, I let it sit for a moment and ponder its color. When the wine is young, it has a lighter pale red color, and when it's aged it turns into reddish brown. Once you realize that different wines have quite different colors, it's fun to discover the different shades of wine and it is quite remarkable how the color can change over time. Wine is a living thing. It matures and evolves in the bottle.

Before I take my first sniff, I swirl the wine in the glass. It helps unleash the aromas in the glass as the wine mingles with air. Pinot Noirs have lovely fruit aromas and always remind me of Grandmother's garden. Sometimes I can smell hints of raspberry in a Pinot Noir, other times hints of cherry or plums. The fruit aromas are stronger when the wine is young. With age they mellow and step back to allow other and subtler flavors to come to the fore.

Smelling less fruit-driven, older Pinot Noirs reminds me of a forest floor, rich smells of the earth, dried leaves, mushrooms, and sometimes even hints of dark chocolate. They are deep and warm smells that make me feel more connected to the earth. Sometimes I smell hints of spices. I am not sure if they remind me of cloves or cinnamon or allspice. Perhaps the smells of a Pinot Noir hover somewhere in between those known smells and take us further into the mystery of what the earth brings forth in such bounty. Herbs and even floral scents can also intermingle with the warmer and heavier smells, but they are even more delicate and subtle. They are like a gentle whisper in the wind.

When you take a sip of a Pinot Noir, it feels light, warm, and smooth at first, but as you let the wine linger on your tongue, it feels enlivening; fruit aromas unfold and a subtle richness lingers as you swallow the wine slowly. It's a feast for the senses. Smells and tastes mingle into one and allow you to savor them in unison. If the wine is well crafted, then I often feel like I am listening to a symphony. Smells of the forest floor elegantly mingle with smells of the orchard and the meadow. My taste buds come to life as the wine slowly glides over the tongue. They awaken from their slumber, and the alcohol alerts them to the magic dance of countless flavors. The warmth of the alcohol joins in with the fresh and tart and zesty acidity encircling the subtle sweetness of the fruit. It is a delicate and supple dance of smells and tastes and textures.

A well-crafted Pinot Noir will unfold its beauty over the course of a meal. To rush through sampling a good Pinot Noir is like missing the trees for the forest. Different nuances waft from the glass and the taste will change over the course of an evening. It's like an open conversation, and the wine will offer different reflections and opinions changed by the food you pair it with and the air the wine "breathes." It invites you into dialogue with its beauty and charm. It helps you open up to be more conversational yourself, to share more openly and reconnect with the world around you. It's a dialogue, and we should not be surprised when experienced wine drinkers

> *"Wine opens the heart.*
> *Opens it! It thaws it right out."*
> **HERMAN MELVILLE**
> **(1819–1891),**
> **AMERICAN NOVELIST**

tell you that a good wine enriches conversations. Wine invites you into a dance of communion where beauty beckons you to open up and share your life with those around you.

Words are inadequate to capture this feast for the senses and the invitation this feast extends. Though the sensations I receive from savoring a glass of wine often hover on the borders of what human language can capture, I can still allow wonder and astonishment to arise within me and open myself up to the world around me.

Enjoying a lovely glass of wine fills my heart with gratitude. For a moment I don't take this gift for granted but marvel that wine exists rather than not. Savoring creates a sanctuary in time and space where I sit still and explore the wonders of creation; I delight in them and I treasure them. They fill my heart with joy.

Too often my fears and anxieties put a layer of heavy dust over the splendors all around me. I can't notice them. Savoring removes the fog in front of my eyes and helps me see more clearly this gift of life that is ours to embrace, to treasure, and to share. As gratitude and joy mingle, I respond to the gifts, and I learn to sit still at his pierced feet. To drink is to pray.

CHAPTER EIGHT

LEARNING ABOUT JOY FROM THE WINE PRESS

All joy wants eternity—wants deep, deep eternity.

FRIEDRICH NIETZSCHE

*G*rowing up on a winery spoils you for life. Perhaps it's more honest to say that growing up in an agricultural community where there is an abundance of fresh food and delicious wine spoils you for life. Though we never had lots of spare money when I was young, we always had an abundance of fresh food from our larger-than-life garden and a wine cellar to turn meals into celebrations. To this day when I savor wines and notice aromas in them, I am taken right back to our family garden and that corner where my grandmother grew our fruit after she "retired" and handed over the responsibility of the winery to a younger generation.

Even when Oma could barely walk anymore, she defied the shackles of old age and whisked her golf cart to our garden just outside the village. There she would shuffle herself on crutches to the garden beds, tending to her beloved plants and watching them grow. Though her life was slowly coming to a close, she still reached out to the seasons of seedtime and harvest, cold and heat, summer and winter, day and night as long as she could. I often felt that Oma was clinging to her very life by joining into the earth's rhythms and harvesting its fruits. The abundance of our garden nurtured her spirit and made her heart sing. It gave her great joy.

Oma grew different varieties of strawberries and raspberries, gooseberries, blackberries, red currants, and black currants. We didn't have just one cherry tree but a black cherry tree, a sour cherry tree, and what I always called our yellowish cherry tree because the cherries remained yellow and light red even when they had ripened. We had peach trees, a wide range of apple trees, and different kinds of pear and plum trees. Dad took an interest in walnut trees and began planting different varieties around the village. I won't even start to write about Oma's massive herb garden or all the veggies she grew.

ABUNDANCE AND JOY

Needless to say there was an abundance and a wide variety of fresh foods. We children learned quickly to become efficient in our family chores and spent what seemed like infinite hours harvesting fruit during the summer months. The rows of strawberries seemed endless, and the raspberry bushes—we children felt with some resentment—could feed the whole village. When one fruit harvest came to an end, another would already be beginning. I especially dreaded harvesting currants. Fiddly clusters of black currants and red currants were never easy to harvest, one small cluster at a time. Sigh. And getting the berries off the stem was even more difficult. *Why did we grow so much fruit?* I often wondered. *It's so much work!*

The flavors of our homegrown fruit and veggies had an intensity and concentration of aromas I rarely taste from produce I buy as a city dweller in the supermarket. I did get spoiled for life, but I didn't know it at the time. I will never forget the smell of a ripe Williams Christ pear and the intense fragrance of our Boskoop apples, so high in vitamin C and so very tart. Our peaches, once fully ripened on the tree, smelled and tasted like paradise to me, so intense and delicious were their aromas. Mom soaked the harvested sour cherries (they did make our lips pucker) in our homemade brandy and stored them for months in an earthen jar. Only toward the winter would the earthen jar reappear, and mom would serve the tipsy cherries with ice cream. The rest of the sour cherries she put in the freezer to make sure we had a good stock to adorn her delicious black forest cake. She only made that cake on special occasions.

Our black currants always had a deep and rich and nearly earthen flavor. Mom usually turned them into concentrated fruit juice. The tart red currants she served with either whipped cream or meringue to balance out the tartness. None of us loved the gooseberries despite the fact that they were loaded with vitamin C. Not only were they very tart but they also had prickly and thick velvety skin and made for a strange experience in the mouth. The texture of goose-berries is a bit of a challenge to the tongue. No one could ever talk us into liking them. Our plums were always the last to ripen. They either joined the sour cherries in the tipsy brandy pot (as we liked to call it) or made their way to adorn our traditional plum tarts, served while still warm with a splash of whipped cream on top. A sprinkling of cinnamon gave them an extra glow. A piece of plum tart with a cup of strong coffee makes for a glorious afternoon splurge, especially after a hard day's labor in the autumn sun.

My favorite season was strawberry season. I remember vividly one particular year when I had long anticipated the ripening of our strawberries. Finally, the first strawberries had turned a deep red and invited us to feast on them. I couldn't wait to get out to our garden after school and pick a handful. I always hunted for the biggest and reddest strawberries. I washed them in the garden well and sat down on the bench by the pond, indulging in these deli-cious, sweet, and intensely fragrant strawberries. Nothing else in the world seemed to matter at that moment; I was so caught up in the pure delight of this sensual pleasure.

One day Oma watched me and took me aside. She pulled me toward a small bed of wild strawberries that I had hardly noticed. They looked a bit shriveled and sad to me, and I never bothered about them. Oma picked one and said, "Try!" I hesitated for a moment, but once I had put the tiny strawberry in my mouth, I was amazed and stunned. The fragrance of this tiny berry was so rich, the sweetness so intense, and the flavor so abundant that I began to marvel. How could such tiny berries carry so much flavor? Why was there such an abundance in such a humble place?

I didn't realize it at the time, but the long summer months spent in our garden are when and where I first learned what it means to savor. They gave me many of the skills and the patience to learn to savor wine, though I didn't know it at the time. On this simple and flat plot of land by the river I learned about the abundance of flavors that the earth can bring forth. I learned to notice them, to name them, and to savor them. A quiet attentiveness to the nuances of flavors and a deep gratitude for the delights of the earth became part of my life. They filled my heart with joy. They taught me to marvel at this life and all the gifts that we receive from the earth. It was only much later I discovered that a small glass of well-crafted wine could mirror all of these delicious and delectable flavors and aromas in concentrated form. It's rather astonishing.

CRUSHED: WINE AND JOY

When I first began sampling wine, I was surprised to discover smells in the wine that were already so familiar to me. I began taking sips of wine at an early age because I was a bit naughty and liked to push against boundaries. In my family children are not allowed to drink any alcohol until the legal age of fourteen, when children are allowed to sample wine under the supervision of their parents. That didn't make any sense to me. Why should I be forbidden to enjoy what the grown-ups drank so freely?

After a wine tasting, when my parents were busy saying goodbye to our guests, I would sneak up and take a tiny little sip from one of the half empty tasting glasses. Oh, it was yummy. I can't remember whether it was really the wine that was so good or the thrill of doing something forbidden.

I loved the Bacchus and Scheurebe wines most when I first began to sample wine as a teenager with my parents around the table. They are a bit like a Sauvignon Blanc. They are fresh and crisp, have lots of fruit aromas, and are easy to drink. It was such a joy when I discovered that they smelled like the black currants in Oma's garden. I felt right at home, and they gave me the feeling that somehow everything is connected and related: the garden, the vineyards, and our wines. Somehow, it made me feel *more* at home. It was comforting and reassuring. It deepened my sense of root-edness, something that I still glean even today when my life so often feels uprooted and in transition.

Many different kinds of wines from all over the world take me right back to that garden of my childhood. When I enjoy an aged Chianti Classico or Chianti Rufina from Tuscany and detect those subtle sour cherry aromas, mellowed over time and blended in with all the other more earthy flavors, I suddenly find myself sitting under our sour cherry tree. It felt like coming home when I first discovered subtle wafts of wild strawberry while sipping a glass of Tempranillo. A distant memory of home mingled with this sensual delight.

When I first sampled a Sauvignon Blanc from New Zealand and noticed asparagus flavors, I found myself yet again back with Oma in our garden, watching her dig into the earth and harvest our delicious white asparagus. White asparagus grows in hiding, deep under the soil. Once there is a little mold on the surface of the soil, it's a sign that the asparagus is shooting up and it's time to dig into the soil and harvest it. How is it that asparagus aromas are found in New Zealand Sauvignon Blanc wines?

It's astounding to me, and the world of wine always surprises and amazes me. It's easy to get used to the bounty of flavors and not be moved by this lavish abundance that meets us in a well-crafted wine. It's tempting to pass over it too quickly. And that's only one of the many delights that wine can bring to us. As I savor wine, I recognize familiar flavors, but the tasting also stirs memories and evokes deep feelings in me. It stirs in me memories of our industrious garden, Oma's larger-than-life presence, and her passion for feeding us so well. "Love goes through the stomach," she would always say.

It also stirs deep feelings in me: feelings of comfort and a profound sense that there will always be enough to feed us. We won't go hungry. If worst comes to worst, if a war should break out again, we can always grow more vegetables in our garden. It's hard to put those feelings into words as they run so deep, but they are reassuring and comforting.

Wine can and will do that to you if you let a wine sing its song. Savoring wine will stir memories in you and evoke emotions that are unique to your own story and invite you to engage life more fully. Just allow the wine to sing its song and to stir you and move you. It just takes time, a willingness to be attentive and go with the flow.

To enjoy wine merely for that instant and immediate sensation of pleasure would be like making love only for the moment of orgasm. There is so much more to the joy that we receive when we savor wine together.

We all long for those moments of delight, pleasure, and deep joy that lift us from the grind of daily existence and make this life more meaningful. Perhaps it's tempting for you to fantasize about what it would be like to grow up on a winery with good wine always in arm's reach. There is nothing romantic about growing up on a winery. It's a stressful existence, especially when your family is involved with every step of the process from planting the vines, growing the grapes, harvesting them, crafting the wine, and selling them to your customers. This life leaves little room for anything else. It's an all-consuming existence. It's hard but deeply rewarding to work with the rhythms of the earth. The moments when we savor the labor of our hands are wonderful, but they are mere moments on that long and laborsome journey of tending to vines, crafting wine, and running a winery. Perhaps our joy of savoring wine is intensified and more complete because the hard labor makes the enjoyment of our wines so much sweeter. It's the knowing and crowning joy of savoring not only the wine but also the fruit of the land, the work of our hands, and the shared passion of crafting something that can bring joy to the world.

The joy that comes from wine is a joy that's gone through the wine press. It's that deep joy we experience when we choose to enter into the cycles of life, death, and new birth, or resurrection as I like to call it. Death always has a share in life even while we are among the living.

> *The joy that comes from wine is a joy that's gone through the wine press.*

I've always been fascinated by our work on the winery, especially harvest season. After many months of hard labor and patient waiting for the autumn sun to chase the last sweetness into the grapes, we harvest those plump and ripe grape clusters. They are a marvelous sight, glowing with life and abundance. And then they are crushed in the wine press. Their skin bursts, and the juice flows like blood. It's quite a violent process. As a child I was always mesmerized watching cluster after cluster being pulled into the crushing and pressing and squeezing of the wine press. The loud noise of the wine press, the churning of the grinding wheels, and the splashing of grape juice was a sight that deeply impressed me. Living yeast bacteria, fungi they call them, begin to hover over these crushed grapes, and slowly a profound process of transformation begins to happen. Only when the grapes are crushed, when the skin has burst and the juice flows, do the fungi begin to do their magical work and slowly transform sticky grape juice into delectable wine.

This process offers a profound analogy for our spiritual lives. Sooner or later we have to come to terms with the fact that if we want to flourish in this life and cultivate joy in our midst, we have to embrace this rhythm of living and dying and being resurrected. It is a sacred rhythm: death brings about spiritual transformation.

It's always tempting to fantasize about having a life without pain, without rejection, without betrayal.

> "The Lord has trodden as in a wine press the virgin daughter Judah. For these things I weep; my eyes flow with tears; for a comforter is far from me."
>
> LAMENTATIONS 1:15-16

To use wine or any other substance to escape the trauma, pain, and even boredom of our lives is to deny ourselves the wonder of learning to flourish in this life. Out of the dance of mirth *and* misery a life lived well is made. When we try to numb the pain within, we also numb our capacity to feel joy. The two go hand in hand. We must not turn away from the hard labor of grieving our losses, of releasing through forgiveness those who have wounded us and learning to receive forgiveness ourselves. We must learn to partake in the great mystery that somehow new life emerges out of dying and letting go. It clears the ground and makes room for new things to grow and flourish. Here we can cultivate joy that far outlasts the instant moments of pleasure, as wonderful as these moments might be.

It's a rhythm all those who want to grow in their spiritual lives must learn. I grew up absorbing my mom's propensity toward anxiety and fear. Perhaps part of my mom's constant need to do things was her desperate attempt to run away from the deep-seated fears inside. Perhaps a whole generation turned to work to soothe the trauma of the war in postwar Germany. I don't know. However, I do know my own fears often run so deep within that they can surface without me even noticing them at first. It's a generational pattern.

When those anxieties and fears rear their ugly head, I have to learn to let them go. They have to die: the fear of the unknown, the anxiety of being rejected, the terror of feeling alone in this world. To face my deepest and darkest fears takes courage. Sometimes I just want to stay with those familiar feelings of anxiety and fear. Somehow, I am at home with them, and stepping out of them seems too frightening. What will be beyond the familiar bog? What will fill these empty spaces in the crevices of my soul?

In those moments of being crushed, when our masks begin to crack and we become more open, vulnerable, and honest about who we really are, new things can begin to grow. Life can emerge out of death.

Like the living and active yeast bacteria hovering over the freshly pressed grape juice, God's life-giving Spirit can hover over us like a mother over her beloved children and comfort and nurture us into the freedom to flourish. Our steps might be small and our progress slow. It's a struggle for sure, but I've learned that this rhythm of life and death and being resurrected into life again can create fertile spiritual soil. Here our pursuit for happiness, our need for immediate pleasure, can be transformed into joy that has learned to love the broken and touch the wounded—in ourselves and in others. The descent into the wine press brings about new wine, rich and vibrant, bringing us joy that outlasts the crushing experiences of life.

> *Like the living and active yeast bacteria hovering over the freshly pressed grape juice, God's life-giving Spirit can hover over us like a mother over her beloved children and comfort and nurture us into the freedom to flourish.*

CHAPTER NINE

CONVIVIAL CELEBRATIONS

Feasts are made for laughter; wine gladdens life.

ECCLESIASTES 10:19

*S*ome of the strongest and most vivid memories of my childhood are all the feasts and celebrations we've had on the winery. Whenever I open a bottle of family wine, faint memories of convivial celebrations awaken, blur into one, and make me feel glad and a little giddy. Past and present merge into one and give me a little emotional lift. They make me smile. Those memories always add a little sweetness to the more bitter and painful memories that have lingered over the years. I hold fast to these sweet memories. They inspire me to take the best of my heritage and share it with those around me.

As I open a chilled bottle of Pinot Blanc, I smell that clear and strong and unpretentious fragrance of our wines. Franconian wines have a good amount of acidity like the Chardonnay wines from the Chablis region in France—those tangy and enlivening acids that awaken your taste buds and make your tongue buzz. The acidity gives the wine structure, and Franconian wines have lots of it. It's that vitality and directness that I so appreciate in our wines. You can't but feel enlivened and refreshed by it, especially during those hot summer months.

> *"Fan the flame of hilarity with the wing of friendship, and pass the rosy wine."*
> CHARLES DICKENS
> (1812–1870),
> ENGLISH NOVELIST

No matter how busy our lives were on the winery, my family eagerly embraced any occasion to have a celebration: birthdays and anniversaries, visits from relatives and friends, baptisms, confirmations, weddings, and of course the feasts of the Christian year: Christmas and New Year, Easter and Pentecost, and we Lutherans even celebrated two saint days, St. Martin on November 11 and St. Nicholas on December 6. With a big family like ours, and relatives nearby, it seemed there was always a reason to celebrate and create a little feast. It seemed rather normal and nothing out of the ordinary to me until I left home.

THE POWER OF CONVIVIALITY

When I left home I suddenly realized how precious those things were that I had taken for granted for most of my life. Only after I had moved abroad to study did I realize that my family's deep love for hospitality and their stamina for long-lasting family celebrations were rather unique. They knew how to mobilize the power of conviviality in their midst. It's an art form and a skill that I treasure to this day and take with me wherever I go.

Sometimes it took days to prepare, sometimes just a day, and most of the time we quickly created a feast out of seemingly nothing. Everyone pitched in. Oma's kitchen was tiny. Looking back I marvel at how she was able to conjure up such amazing meals in her humble kitchen. Mom's kitchen wasn't big either, but there was more space for us to help, and we had a decent-sized table right in the kitchen. It meant there were often other people sitting around the kitchen table, chopping and chatting and sipping a glass of wine in anticipation of the feast to come.

Despite all the family tensions and Oma's often overbearing presence, there always was the sense that we belong to one another, no matter what. We stuck together and embraced the feasts as they came—small and great, short and long, simple and elaborate.

Thankfully, we didn't have Martha Stewart magazines hovering over our imagination like sugar candy, pink and puffy clouds obscuring our vision and making us feel inadequate about our cooking and decorating skills. We had to work with what our garden offered, and we kept things simple. There was great freedom in that. You don't need that much to create a little feast.

When I moved to the United States, I found many of my friends felt too intimidated to have people over. They didn't feel their house was nice enough, or they didn't feel they could cook well enough, or they didn't know how to pick out a wine they thought would please the guests. The stress they felt made me sad. Why do we put so much pressure on ourselves and make what should be happy and lighthearted occasions into acts of performance, competition, and feats of perfectionism?

THE IMPERFECT HOST

I grew up in a house built in the middle of the seventeenth century. For most of its life, it served as a storehouse for grains. The upper-level floors are topsy-turvy because of it. Heavy sacks of grain slowly eroded the stone floors and made them crack. The walls of most rooms are crooked, and our bathroom is tiny. Put that together with our normal family interactions, and it quickly became obvious to the outsider that they were not dealing with a perfect family. But that was okay, and we still had lots of people over. Somehow, they didn't mind that we weren't perfect. On the contrary, sometimes I think that's precisely what drew them to us.

The staircase to our home, I do have to admit, is impressive. It has steep stone steps with antlers hanging from the sidewalls going along the steps, revealing our family's love affair with game.

Wild boar, venison, and wild rabbit were staples in our home, though I wasn't so sure about the wild rabbit. I could never be convinced that it really was the delicacy my parents made it out to be. Game was inexpensive, full of flavor, and lean. You can't argue with that. If you have a chance to try wild boar with a lovely aged Chianti from Tuscany, it's a delicious combination. Wild boar is actually a specialty in Tuscany.

As the roast sizzles in the oven, add some sour cherries and a little bitter chocolate to the gravy. These deep and rich flavors resound the flavors in the Chianti wine, and in no time you have a little symphony going on. It's not that difficult. Venison goes well with the more savory and less fruit-laden Pinot Noirs from Burgundy, France, Oregon, or Central Otago, New Zealand. Oregonians enjoy wild salmon with their lovely Pinot Noirs, a combination that surprised me at first, and now I love it. That's the wonderful thing about matching food with wine. There will always be surprises if you allow yourself to experiment and develop your palette.

Game isn't everyone's cup of tea, of course, so Mom made sure to cook meat that pleased the popular palette. I always got to set the table, and tablecloths came out only for very special occasions. While Mom was busy in the kitchen, Dad went to the cellar to pick out the wines. As guests poured into our small kitchen, the noise level increased and things became more chaotic. Mom maneuvered everyone to the dining table in the small living room. We made sure Oma sat on the opposite end of the table from Mom, surrounded by two of her grandchildren, keeping her occupied, distracted, and cared for. The stage was set and the feast could begin.

My parents learned the art of cultivating the power of conviviality from their parents. It was part of the culture they grew up in, and they chose to make it their own. It doesn't take much to cultivate a joyous atmosphere, but there is a definite cultural knowledge and skill to it. You can't force or rush it. That will most likely kill it. Perfectionism is unfertile soil for conviviality. Try to relax and be yourself, which is okay and actually most inviting—unless you're in a bad mood. That won't help your guests feel welcome and comfortable.

You create and hold a space in which food and wine can do their magic. Slowly but surely lively conversations gain momentum and transform a wide assortment of guests into a profoundly cheerful party. It's an amazing gift. I find it difficult to capture in words that wonderfully sacred dynamic when grace—those supersurplus gifts—somehow reaches deeply into the crevices of our lives and draws us into a space of festive play and even wonder.

If you want to see grace at work around the table, just watch the film *Babette's Feast*. It's not an action film; it invites you into a contemplative place. Don't be intimidated by the extravagant meal in the film. It's to create a contrast with the severely ascetical guests accustomed to scarcity. It's the one film that, to me, captures in the most moving way how conviviality gains momentum and transforms a divided and uptight religious group of people into a merry party. I weep every time I see it. I have come to know deeply the truth of the film. I believe in its goodness, and we should not deprive ourselves of such divine gifts, such moments of unexpected graces.

Because we had grown up on a winery, joyous celebrations were a natural and regular part of our lives. Wine begs and invites and calls upon merry moods even when we don't feel like it. Those celebrations often lifted us out of the grind of daily existence, easing our burdens that some days just felt too hard to carry. And wine played a unique part in all of it. The food was always delicious but mostly simple. We never had much spare time for these preparations, and they mostly happened on the side. In the summer months we often had grilled meat. Dad would start up the grill on the run, finishing up last chores that needed to be done that day. Mom made her delicious potato salad. Oma contributed the tomato salad and fresh berries arranged on a crumbly tart. We children learned early how to make the perfect dressing for our fresh lettuce with lots of chopped chives sprinkled on top. It was mostly simple but home-grown food with an abundance of flavors, sometimes subtle, sometimes intense and rich. And the wine added a dimension that transformed our family gatherings into feasts and celebrations, even the humble ones. As we gathered and the power of conviviality was unleashed, people kept lingering and mingling, firming up bonds of kinship and friendship—even at those times when we were struggling to get along.

> *"Over a bottle of wine many a friend is found."*
> **YIDDISH PROVERB**

There can be great beauty in food and there can be great beauty in wine. When these two are brought together in pleasing ways, offered by a gracious and generous host, they seem to double and triple their effect. They seem to bring delight and pleasure in ways that make it hard for people to resist their allure. They chisel away at our defenses and crumble our resistances. They invite us to linger. I've noticed how guests find it hard to leave, so they stay for a little while longer. It's in the staying and the lingering and the savoring that soulful things happen. The intensity of conversations and the prolonged times of laughter gather momentum and turn into something yet more beautiful. A giddiness descends on the party and keeps everyone in its spell until it gathers to such great happiness that the positive energy spills over to even the most reserved and stressed of the party.

Such joyful celebrations create a space for deeper bonding and untangling knots. It's a space where sharing personal and vulnerable things becomes more inviting as people gather up the courage to be brave. We move to new levels of knowing and being known in the midst of the tensions of our fractured lives. Somehow it seems easier to let go of hurt and resentment, of bitterness and pain, and to embrace one another in a generosity of spirit that has learned to forgive and let go. Martin Buber once wrote that everything real in life is encounter. To me those celebrations always seemed real. They never plastered over the raw stuff that my family struggled with, but they allowed us to move beyond it, knowing that some things change very slowly.

THE TRANSFORMATIVE JOY
OF WINE AND FOOD

The beauty in a well-crafted wine is different from the beauty in food. When we pick a ripe raspberry or a tomato or chives, the flavor is right there. It's immediate, straightforward, and a fairly simple love affair. It's different with wine. The manifold flavors in a wine are only unleashed in and through fermentation. Once the grape juice has been fermented into wine and the flavors are unleashed, it's the alcohol that holds, preserves, and matures the flavor in the wine. Carefully crafted wines have the natural potential for a concentration of beauty and flavors that gather up the bounty of creation in most mysterious ways. Wine, like no other food, can capture and preserve the beauty of a particular place in the fullness of time and invite us to savor it. It's marvelous. It's an altogether different love affair. Fragrances from fruit orchards to grassy meadows to herb gardens and forest floors merge into one and enchant those who have learned to savor. The process of fermentation and the resulting alcohol gather this greatness and offer it to us as an undeserved gift. Calling wine an "alcoholic beverage" misses the point of wine. Wine is bottled poetry. The alcohol is the music the wine dances to.

> *Wine is bottled poetry. The alcohol is the music the wine dances to.*

And just as the alcohol makes the flavors of the wine come alive and dance, it also invites us to the dance of savoring. It stirs and moves us in ways that food can't. The alcohol carries the aromas to our noses and alerts our taste buds to the delights to come. Yes, once we've had too much alcohol, it dulls the senses. But the slow delight of savoring will open up our senses to notice subtle delights more fully.

Oma was always the first to show signs of happiness. As Dad served her a glass of sparkling wine made from the Pinot Blanc grape, it's as if the bubbles began to dissolve some of the tension she always seemed to carry. Her cheeks would turn a soft red, and her eyes brightened. We could tell when her body began to relax and she let go of that serious and piercing look that seemed to judge the world around her. I well remember when I first lifted a glass of sparkling wine to my mouth and my nose felt the sparkles. Once I took the first sip, I felt the bubbles dancing on my tongue. It was a funny sensation, really, but absolutely lovely. Oma has always had a great smile, but with every sip she took of the sparkling wine, she smiled a little more. Together with Oma, everyone else began to relax into the feast to come.

Mom still would be buzzing around the kitchen, placing food on the table, and getting last-minute things done. But when Dad settled into his place at the table and served the wine to go along with the food, things settled down. As he poured the light, golden liquid of our lovely Silvaner wine, conversations became more animated and hands reached out to platters and bowls, filling plates with generous servings. Once Mom had carved the roast, she also would begin to relax into the moment. When she finally joined us and settled down on her chair, things really took off.

Mom's roasts were always amazing. Crisp and crunchy skin surrounded the juicy and tender center of her pork roasts. The herbs gave the meat a lovely savory fragrance. The potatoes from our garden had a deep yellow color, and their texture was dense and rich. When Dad had served everyone their wine and was able to take his first bite, you could visibly see how he was easing into the comfort of food and wine. For a little

> *"What's all this hiding happiness and wine away? I've lined up with the libertines now, come what may."*
>
> HAFEZ
> (C. 1315–1390),
> PERSIAN POET

while he left behind all his worries and responsibilities of running a winery and was able to let go and give himself to the bliss of the moment. The Silvaner, with its strong acidity and savory fragrance, cuts right through the fat of the roast and complements the rich flavors of the pork very well indeed. They are good company.

Alcohol enters the bloodstream rather quickly. I do believe the triple effect of delicious food, delectable wine, and the potent powers of alcohol helps soften the hard places and makes us more tender toward one another. Suddenly, Dad wouldn't mind so much that his four daughters were lively and loud and, yes, at times rather obnoxious. Perhaps the fate of having four daughters and no son seemed a little less daunting. Dealing with budding teenage girls is an art form, and lots of grace was needed. As we were listening to the clinking of our wine glasses, that lovely sound of togetherness, the tensions in all of us would ease and bring us together, despite the fact that we sometimes felt like strangers to one another. These feasts and convivial celebrations are deeply imprinted on my imagination. They lifted us out of the demanding grip and grind of running a winery and brought us together as a family. The wine intoxicated us enough to allow us a glimpse into the heart of things. Perhaps the wine helped to remove the fog of our cares and see a bit more clearly. In those moments of festive play I learned to marvel at the joys that emerge from within when we realize that to be alive is a wondrous gift.

CHAPTER TEN

WINE, SEX, AND GOD

Let him kiss me with the kisses of his mouth!
For your love is better than wine.

Song of Songs 1:2

*P*erhaps you feel surprised that I should reflect on how wine can enhance our sex lives.

The breakdown of marriages, and therefore family life, in our societies is a painful and daunting reality. There are no easy solutions as the pressures on marriages and family life continue to gain momentum. It's not easy to connect and be in sync with one another. And when we do find the time to connect, we might have very different expectations of one another. One partner may want to talk more while the other might want to get on with things and have sex. That's where wine can come in and help bridge the gap. Wine is a great compromise: it stimulates conversation and gets the body ready for the pleasures to come.

It is a well-known fact that alcohol enjoyed in moderation functions as a blood thinner and increases the blood flow of the body, which is of course beneficial for getting sexually aroused. But did you know that drinking wine stimulates the same parts of the brain as having sex? It's a complex process, and researchers in the neurosciences are still trying to figure it all out.

However, we do know for sure that the smell of wine also functions as a stimulant. Our olfactory receptor cells pick up the scents that travel through our noses and the retronasal passage and report it to the same part of our brain that processes emotions and memories and somehow releases them into freer flow. Emotions are a key mediator of sexual desire, which in turn helps prepare the body to get sexually aroused.

And particular scents are known to sexually arouse us. They vary for women and men and from culture to culture and depend greatly on previous experiences we've had and the memories we associate with them. Some are aroused by the warm scents of wood, earth, and musk, and others by vanilla, caramel, cinnamon, allspice, and licorice, and still others by the scent of cherry, lavender, strawberry, or even chocolate. What will arouse one might not do much to another. We have to get to know our own bodies (and noses) and what scents (and wines) might help our dance of intimacy. An aged Chianti Classico, made from the Sangiovese grape in Tuscany, has a lot of the smells known to stimulate sexual desire.

A recent scientific survey seems to confirm that the moderate consumption of red wine might well enhance our sex lives. It's not surprising to me that the Italians discovered it. We Germans, industrious and efficient as we often are, sometimes look longingly at our Italian neighbors, who seem to have mastered the enjoyment of earthly pleasures.

To return to the study, it was medical doctors from the University of Florence, nestled in the enchanting Chianti region of Tuscany, who recruited nearly eight hundred women ages eighteen to fifty for a survey in 2009. They found that women who consumed between one and two glasses of red wine scored higher on the female sexual-function index than those who did not drink or consumed other alcoholic beverages. It seems that enjoying one to two glasses of red wine affects women's sexual desire, lubrication (think blood flow), and overall sexual function in rather positive ways.

Considering all of this, it might not be a bad idea at all for couples to take some time to sit and sip a well-crafted wine and see where things go from there. Wine as a social lubricant takes on a whole new dimension when thought of in relation to our sex lives.

AMBIVALENT FEELINGS LINGER

The church hasn't always been enthusiastic about bringing wine and sex together. When we look at the history of Western art, we find many paintings warning the onlooker that wine is primarily a dangerous means of seduction. And St. Augustine of Hippo, one of the most influential early theologians of the Western church, wrote some gloomy essays on sex and why it is so dangerous. I once read through these essays because I was looking for a quote by Augustine on the pleasures of wine. It was a depressing read, to say the least. He and his contemporaries set a frame of mind that has haunted the Western church ever since. Though Martin Luther and many Reformers praised sex as a gift from God and openly expressed their delight in nuptial bliss and even made their wedding night a political spectacle, their message did not get carried forward. To this day Protestants and Catholics alike have continued to struggle to find a constructive way forward.

> *"He who loves not wine, women and song remains a fool his whole life long."*
>
> **MARTIN LUTHER**
> **(1483–1546),**
> **GERMAN THEOLOGIAN**
> **AND REFORMER**

And yet since ancient times, wine has been known to enhance our sex lives, and the delights of sex and wine are often compared to one another. The Bible is no exception in this regard. The Song of Songs celebrates sex, like wine, as a gift from God with such natural grace and vivid imagery that it makes the stoic blush and the ascetic deny its literal meaning.

Sex unites lovers physically, emotionally, and spiritually. The ecstasy of erotic love is a great gift to humanity, and yet many struggle with this dance of intimacy. Humans need help, and wine has offered it throughout the ages. Wine helps to relax, to let go of anxieties, stress, and weariness of spirit; arouses the senses; and opens the heart for the other. Wine helps to break down barriers and prepares body and soul for the pleasures to come.

The Song of Songs reflects unashamedly about the yearning and wooing of lovers, the waiting and longing, the speaking of sweet words and the utter delights of arousal and nuptial bliss. Come and listen in on some of these beautiful musings: "Your love is sweeter than wine," exclaims the lady. "He leads me into the wine cellar /and his banner over me is love.... His left arm rests under my head / and his right hand embraces me" (Song of Songs 1:2; 2:4, 6 author's translation). He woos her with sweet words of his delight in her body: "How beautiful you are, my love, / how very beautiful! ... Your lips are like a crimson thread, / and your mouth is lovely.... Your two breasts are like two fawns, / twins of a gazelle, / that feed among the lilies.... You have ravished my heart.... How much better is your love than wine.... A garden locked is my sister, my bride" (Song of Songs 4:1, 3, 5, 9, 10, 12). She invites him in: "Let my beloved come to his garden, / and eat its choicest fruits" (Song of Songs 4:16). He does not linger but enters his garden and drinks deeply from the wine he finds there and becomes drunk with love (Song of Songs 5:1).

The Song of Songs stands in a long tradition of erotic love poems, and writers throughout the ages have continued to celebrate wine and sex as wonderful gifts to humanity. Why not take this book of the Bible literally and allow wine to take its rightful place in our midst once again?

What is so beautiful about the Song of Songs is that it is smack in the middle of the Bible and thereby embeds the enjoyment and delights of sex and wine into our journey of faith. Our faith should help us and enable us to enjoy these gifts from God both with freedom and in the safety of loving covenant relationships.

Sex, like wine, can and should become a place where the boundaries between earthly and heavenly pleasures blur and where the ecstasy of erotic love elevates the lovers to the even more ecstatic and eternal love of God. Union with one another at its best should lead us into deeper union with God. While you won't necessarily hear this in Sunday school, it is safe to say that the Song of Songs celebrates nuptial delights as a gift from God and sees it as part of our journey to the heavenly wedding banquet.

> "Wine prepares the heart for love unless you take too much. It warms the blood, adds luster to the eyes, And wine and love have ever been allies."
>
> OVID
> (43 BC–AD 17),
> ROMAN POET

It is time to expand our vision of our spiritual lives to include understanding wine and sex as spiritual gifts from our benevolent Creator. We need to learn to shed and let go of any negative feelings about sex that might hover in the deep crevices of our souls. Shame in particular is an emotion that has hovered over many Christians, especially women, and its impact echoes back over many centuries.

It is not going to be an easy fix, but let me assure you, over time, with one glass of well-crafted wine in the one hand and a good translation of the Song of Songs in the other, you will be well on your way. You will discover the delights of wine and sex can bring a holy playfulness to your marriage that is loving, caring, and respectful toward the other, just like the Song of Songs sings it.

CHAPTER ELEVEN

WINE, HEALTH, AND HEALING

Ripe, good old wine imparts a richer blood
To him who daily tastes its tonic flood.

MEDICAL SCHOOL OF SALERNO,
CODE OF HEALTH, ELEVENTH CENTURY

Since ancient times, people have explored the healing properties of wine. You would be surprised to learn how much the Greeks, the Romans, the Persians, and medieval monks and nuns researched the various healing properties of wine and carefully documented them for future generations. Today wine is being rediscovered as a healing agent, especially as we look for more natural remedies to overcome our overdependence on pharmaceutical drugs.

Our bodies and souls are in constant need of healing and restoration. After a long day's work, people come home to recover and restore themselves for yet another long day at work. I don't recommend relying on alcohol to help you relax, and you certainly don't want to drown your stress and sorrow in wine. However, a glass of well-crafted wine can sure help you step out of the treadmill of a highly competitive and stressful work environment and help you relax into a mode of being that is more saturated with grace, levity, and beauty.

> *"No longer drink only water, but take a little wine for the sake of your stomach and your frequent ailments."*
>
> 1 TIMOTHY 5:23

Perhaps the most healing approach to enjoying a glass of wine is with a posture of gratitude. Gratitude doesn't always come naturally to me. It's hard sometimes for me to pin down what keeps me from leaning into a posture of gratitude and the seeds of joy it plants in my soul.

FROM PERFECTIONISM TO GRATITUDE

Alexander Schmemann, a wise and seasoned theologian, once said that perfectionism kills joy. He believes we have embraced the modern ethos of a joyless and business-minded culture, and our frantic hunger and thirst for perfection is the death of joy. These words struck a deep cord within me and have haunted me ever since I first read them.

It took me a long time to even understand what perfectionism is. When you are in the rut of it, it seems just the normal way to live. When it comes down to it, perfectionism is the fear of one's own failures and shortcomings, and more profoundly the fear of losing the approval and love of those we seek to please. When we are haunted by a sense of perfectionism, it's as if we drive through life with our hand brake on. It suffocates our inner freedom to blossom and flourish in life. There is no grace in perfectionism, and it's the antithesis of the Christian life, in which we know ourselves loved and embraced in the midst of our shortcomings.

I grew up in a culture where many things are set to a high standard: our educational system, our public services, our engineering—just think about those smoothly running and reliable German cars or our strong economy! Yes, it's impressive, but it comes at a high price. Though I have never heard it said out loud, there is a subtle and strong current within my culture that makes us believe that perfection is a goal we can actually reach. It's no wonder that many of us have ingested deep compulsions toward trying to be perfect and perpetually working ourselves into a frenzy. It's a stressful way to live, and there is not much room for grace in it, but it sure helps the person who wants to be a productive, efficient, and successful individual.

There is nothing wrong with setting high standards, but when the undercurrent of life becomes obsessed with getting it right and joy erodes into anxiety or, worse, despair, perhaps it's time to take a step back. That's what I had to do. I had to learn to be intentional about setting up practices that help me slow down in order to cultivate gratitude and joy. We should never use wine and alcohol to drown our frustrations and anxieties about not being able to measure up. That is not what wine is for. That's when we should open up life to receive help from those whose wisdom can set us free.

The evenings are often a time when I settle into a more quiet space and reflect on the day. Sometimes I pour myself a glass of wine and reflect on the good things that happened throughout the day, and I try to release the difficult things into God's hands. As the aromas of the wine stir my senses and as the alcohol warms my body, I settle into a more relaxed mode. I use this time to pause and say thank you.

> *"Wine, one sip of this will bathe the drooping spirits in delight beyond the bliss of dreams. Be wise and taste."*
>
> JOHN MILTON
> (1608–1674),
> ENGLISH POET

It's a simple ritual, but the glass of wine in my hand reminds me of God's goodness. No matter what my day was like, I try to sink into the comfort of being held by God. Sometimes—well, let's be honest, often—I am disappointed with what I have been able to accomplish. Then I try to defy the spirit of perfectionism by raising my glass, cheering to God's benevolence, and having a laugh at my incessant to-do lists. In wine there is grace, and out of our experience of grace flow gratitude and joy.

HEALING THE BODY AND THE SOUL

Only after we have learned to enjoy wine with wisdom and in moderation can we understand why wine has been celebrated and elevated as medicine. Wine can move us into a more soulful existence and can help heal our bodies and improve our physical health. Since ancient times wine has been used as a medicine and was the primary medicine until the nineteenth century. Did you know that the moderate consumption of wine can help reduce the risk of cardiovascular diseases? In many Western countries cardiovascular diseases are the leading cause of death, so this is no small matter.

But what many don't realize is that wine, enjoyed in the company of others, has health benefits far greater and more encompassing than just our physical health. Too often when we trek to the doctor, we are examined for physical ailments, but the emotional and spiritual dimensions of our lives often go unexamined and unnoticed. And yet we all know that our emotional pain can easily manifest in our bodies, and our bodies hold and carry so much of the tension and stress we feel and endure. I come from a family that was not good at noticing, naming, and dealing with negative emotions. I am better at it now, but it's often my body that tells me that I am stressed or hurting and that I need to pay attention to matters of the soul.

I vividly remember reading through the letters of spiritual counsel by the great German Reformer Martin Luther, and I was so surprised how down-to-earth and practical he was in his advice. One of his letters is written to a troubled and depressed friend. Luther, who struggled with anxiety and depression himself, gets right to the point and tells his friend that he needs to get himself out of his isolation, seek the company of others, and enjoy a glass

> *"Sorrow can be alleviated by good sleep, a bath and a glass of good wine."*
>
> THOMAS AQUINAS
> (C. 1225–1274),
> ITALIAN THEOLOGIAN

of wine with them. It was so refreshing to read and helped me remember how therapeutic it is to share a glass of wine in the company of friends.

We should not underestimate how a glass of wine shared with family and friends and seasoned with conversation can bring relief from physical, emotional, and even spiritual stress. Brooding moods can easily cage us. Negative thought patterns are destructive, and in no time we spiral down into the abyss of catastrophic thinking. Stepping out, meeting up with friends, and sipping a glass of wine is a great way to help us escape melancholy moods and lean into conviviality and joy together.

Not only does wine in moderation have soothing, warming, and relaxing effects on the body, it also helps us be more courageous and vulnerable, allowing others to get a glimpse into our troubles and help carry our burdens. When we are down, we are tempted to withdraw from the world. Who wants to admit to struggling and feeling low? But exactly at these points in our lives we need to seek out the company of caring friends and delight in the gifts of God to whisk us out of fallow moods. It's not surprising that Proverbs instructs us to give strong drink to one who is perishing and wine to those in bitter distress, so they can forget about their troubles for a little while and not be pulled down into the abyss of despair (Proverbs 31:6-7).

> "Give strong drink to one who is perishing, and wine to those in bitter distress; let them drink and forget their poverty, and remember their misery no more."
>
> PROVERBS 31:6-7

WINE AND THE ART OF AGING

Aging well is an art form, and wine can bring comfort and strength to the aging. It takes courage to look beyond the fears of aging and death. It's a hard reality to face that our bodies will become more fragile, our minds less reliable, and even the most energetic will feel their energy levels dropping and slipping away. No one likes to be weak, but all of us at one point or another will have to come to terms with our human frailty. Blessed are those who are surrounded by a loving community to journey with them into old age.

I remember vividly as a child reading *Little Red Riding Hood*, one of my favorite Grimm's Fairy Tales. In the story, the mother sends Little Red Riding Hood on a mission: "Come, Little Red Riding Hood, here is a piece of cake and a bottle of wine. Take them to your grandmother, she is ill and weak, and they will do her good." I often felt right at home in these fairy tales because they connected me with real life, with things that I experienced as a child. My grandmother was frail and old, and my parents often sent me to bring her comfort. After Grandpa had died, I often stayed at her place to keep her company. She lived just across the courtyard from us. One of my "chores" was to warm her bed at night. When Grandma was ready to go to bed, I got out of hers and slipped into my own bed beside her bed. Another way to comfort her was to make sure that Grandmother always had a small supply of wine, even when she was so frail that she had to go to a care home. I think it brought her great comfort to sip a glass of wine in the lonely evenings at the dusk of her life. When we share a glass of wine with those who are aging, their comfort is doubled.

The medicinal properties of wine go far beyond the healing of the body and allow our souls to dwell in more pleasant pastures when the sorrows of life seem to crowd in and cloud over our vision. The beauty of a well-crafted wine can baptize our imagination and help us see beyond the constraints of the day and give us the courage to embrace hope in the midst of the sorrows that this life will surely bring.

CHAPTER TWELVE

FROM INTIMIDATION
TO APPRECIATION

Wine reveals who we are or who we want and pretend to be. It has
become an agent of pretension and snobbery, an agent of deception.

JONATHAN NOSSITER, PARAPHRASED

*Y*ou might think that all this talk about the enjoyment of
wine sounds nice, but what about those of us who are new
to the wine world, who haven't grown up with wine or don't know
much about it? It's true, the wine world has become incredibly
complex. To many, this world seems intimidating and elitist. How
are we to find our way through the maze of wine choices? And
what about all that wine talk? It seems like we have to learn a

whole new language in order to enter this world, become an insider, and keep up with the lingo. For something that is intended to bring us joy, that seems like a whole load of added homework and pressure to perform. All we wanted is to relax with a glass of wine!

When the uninitiated walk into the wine section of a good supermarket or into a wine shop, they can't help but feel overwhelmed by all the choices. Rows and rows of wine seem like an impenetrable world to the newcomer. Wine countries, wine regions, grape varieties, and wine accessories blur into one impenetrable maze. Would you like white, red, or rosé wine? Do you prefer champagne, prosecco, or sparkling wine made méthode traditionnelle? Have you tried port, sherry, or brandy? Does your wine bottle have a screw cap or cork? If you prefer wines with cork, make sure you have a good selection of corkscrews, foil cutters, and cork retrievers at hand. Would you like to decant or aerate your wine? Make sure you use the right wine glass for the wine you purchased. And we haven't even looked at the wine labels yet. That's a whole world in itself, and it seems like we need a university degree to learn how to read them. Yes, the wine world has become incredibly complex.

Now don't get me wrong. Today it is possible to have access to wonderful and high-quality wines from around the world. In many ways we are in a golden age of wine. But it's still hard to know how to penetrate this world and figure out what you like and how much you have to spend to get a decent bottle of wine.

Many of my friends decided they are not interested in wine because they feel they can't penetrate the wine world and keep up with it. They feel it's something for the upper middle class and intellectuals, the well-to-do, so to speak. They wouldn't know where to begin, and feelings of inadequacy hover right below the surface. It brings up deep insecurities within them. Why? Is it just a personal problem of theirs?

No, it's actually a widespread experience and a byproduct of the way we talk about and present wine today. Somehow the way wine is presented today seems to elicit or tap into feelings of inadequacy and intimidation very quickly. It makes me sad. It shouldn't be that way. I often wonder what happened to the world of wine that it seems to elicit such confusing and negative feelings in so many people.

> *"To exalt, enthrone,*
> *establish and defend,*
> *To welcome home*
> *mankind's mysterious friend*
> *Wine, true begetter*
> *of all arts that be;*
> *Wine, privilege of*
> *the completely free;*
> *Wine the recorder; wine*
> *the sagely strong;*
> *Wine, bright avenger*
> *of sly-dealing wrong,*
> *Awake, . . . [Divine] Muse,*
> *and sing the vineyard song!"*
>
> HILAIRE BELLOC
> (1870–1953),
> FRENCH ENGLISH
> POET AND WRITER

THE MARKETING WORLD

There are many reasons for this change, but one of them is that we live in consumer societies with intense and unrelenting competition. The marketing world sees us primarily as shoppers, and its marketing machines are to ensure that we stay put in our compliant roles as obedient consumers. Companies compete with one another for our attention and ultimately our money, our spending power. They know how easily we feel insecure, inadequate, and intimidated. They stir those feelings within us. Then they use them to make us spend money and buy stuff so we feel we can fit in and somehow belong.

The intimidation and inadequacy we feel when we walk into a wine shop or the wine section of a supermarket are not accidental, random, or simply part of our natural emotional makeup. They are purposefully created within us. Highly paid marketing experts have spent precious time analyzing consumer behavior and how to manipulate it. First, they create an environment that will exacerbate any feelings of intimidation and inadequacy we might already have. In supermarkets it will be the seemingly endless and overwhelming choices of wines from all over the world with little guidance for the consumer on how to maneuver within it. Once these feelings are created or deepened, supermarkets will then offer us a path through the maze.

Aware that the average customer knows little about wine, they will present to us "special offers" to help us make a "discerning" purchase. These "special offers" will help ease our feelings of intimidation and inadequacy as they provide some guidance through the maze. As we study the wine on offer and realize that the "regular" price is much higher, we increasingly feel that we are making a good choice by outsmarting the system and purchasing a really good bottle of wine for only half of its original price. We are now convinced that we are getting a real bargain. Altogether the experience becomes emotionally satisfying. We arrived at the supermarket feeling somewhat lost and bewildered, and we leave with the feeling that we have a real bargain in hand.

The fact that these wines are often not worth the money we spent doesn't matter. The amount of bland and uninspiring wines we can find in supermarkets and the fact that wines from different parts of the world can taste so similar nowadays seem rather disappointing to me. The marketing experts know that most customers don't know enough to judge the quality of the wine. More often than not, they have enticed us to spend more money on cheap and industrially made wine because their ultimate goal is profit. Now, this scheme is not true for all supermarkets and all wine offers, but for the most part I have found these special promotions questionable at best. I don't trust them. We might be disappointed with the wine once we open the bottle, but we will then be tempted to think that we just don't know enough about wine to judge its quality. Perhaps we are even tempted to give up on wine altogether.

We have to remember that in highly competitive consumer societies, those who control the behavior of consumers have much power. The subtle and not so subtle messages of the marketing world are like strings attached to a puppet. They want to make us dance according to their tunes, tunes primarily oriented toward profit and often inspired by pure greed. The impression they give us is that the world is there for us to consume and enjoy, but they really want to make us blindly and willingly buy their products so they can make more profit.

It's a tricky world out there, and wine has not been spared of it. Supermarkets are only one part of the equation. Specialty wine stores, wine boutiques, and wine bars are popping up everywhere.

Increasingly, advertisements present wine as an end in itself, a means by which we secure a sense of identity and belonging to a certain class of society, a way to differentiate ourselves from the masses. If we can afford to buy certain wines and, even better, if we have acquired a certain way of talking about wine, then we have earned a place in an esteemed group of wine lovers and experts. It's comforting to know that we belong, but make sure to keep up. It's easy to fall behind.

Yes, the wine world not only feels exclusive, but wine is often used today to create a sense of exclusivity. Too often wine has become a status symbol, a mark of our education, our sophistication, and our wealth. Through wine we can now secure for ourselves an esteemed place in society. It's often a subtle process but very real indeed. Especially when we are new to this world, we feel keenly how ill-prepared we are to enter into it. With no background to know how to engage the world of wine, we are left to the schemes of the marketing world, vulnerable to how they formulate and dictate the newly invented rules of the wine game. Be alert and don't give in. We don't have to play their games or be confined by their rules.

There are other, more liberating ways to understand and enjoy wine. Wine has been around for thousands of years, and people from all walks of life have enjoyed wine, often without much knowledge about it. We don't actually need to know a lot about wine to enjoy it. I think that's good news for us. I would like to create a space where you can explore the world of wine with a sense of freedom that you don't have to measure up or compete. I would like to help you develop an attitude of carefree curiosity and learn to trust your own palate.

CONTEMPORARY WINE TALK

As you listen in to conversations about wine or read an article written by a professional wine writer, please keep in mind that contemporary wine talk is still a recent phenomenon. For the last forty to fifty years, a way of speaking and writing about wine has emerged and developed that has done two important things. On the one hand, it has helped open our vision to the amazing and manifold wonders of the world of wine, such as the many different grape varieties and their particular flavors, their origins, and their regional particulars. Never before have we been able to explore the flavors of wine in such detail and with such expertise. The attention devoted to the particulars of the smell, taste, and texture of wine is astounding, and the amount of writing on the subject matter beyond compare. That's the good news. If you have the intellectual curiosity, the spare pocket money, and enough leisure time to explore it, you will find yourself kept busy, engaged, and entertained for the rest of your days.

The challenging bit is that this new wine-writing guild has emerged within a highly competitive consumer culture and often perpetuates its problems. It is a hierarchical world and has become extremely competitive. Wine writers have to compete with one another for the attention of their readers. They acquire highly specialized knowledge about wine, often in a very short period of time, and through it exercise power as they influence and shape the opinions of consumers looking for guidance in this ever-more-complex world of wine. The general assumption is that in order to truly appreciate wine, you have to become an insider and learn to talk about wine the way they do. Considering that people have enjoyed wine for thousands of years without this highly analytical, descriptive, and prescriptive way of speaking about wine flavors, I think it's time to take a step back and get some perspective.

It dawned on me a few years ago how this way of approaching and introducing wine not only sets up barriers but also keeps people from discovering the manifold gifts of wine for themselves. I thought about it again when I was doing an event about the spirituality of wine for a fantastic wine shop in Seattle.

The shop was wine heaven for me. A thoughtful selection of delicious and quite affordable wines from some of my favorite wine regions was on display. I don't tend to get intimidated by it all. I have learned to be okay with the fact that my knowledge about wine is limited and am always happy to find someone who can help me out. I felt like a little girl in a candy shop and skipped up and down the rows of wine, delighting in the fantastic selection and in the thoughtfulness of the person who had selected those wines. The master of the house was traveling, and he had put others in charge during his absence.

We were a small group, and after I did a presentation on the spirituality of wine, I wanted to lead the group into wine tasting as a spiritual practice. I wanted to help them discover how savoring wine can connect them to God as the Creator and Giver of the bountiful gifts of creation. My plan was to help my guests experience how tasting and savoring wine can become part of cultivating an embodied spirituality where the enjoyment of wine can open up new ways of drawing near to God and communing with him.

But there was a problem. The wine shop decided to let their youngest employee introduce the wines to us. Now, I tell organizers that I want as little introduction to the wines as possible because I want people to learn to explore the wines for themselves. I want to protect them from the onslaught of a massive amount of detailed information that will make them easily give up on trusting their own encounter with the wine.

Perhaps my request got lost in translation or I forgot to mention it. I can't remember, but I realized quickly that this young man was ready for battle. He had read all the right books, acquired a high degree of proficiency in contemporary wine lingo, and had prepared his presentation well in advance. Swinging his newly acquired knowledge like a sword in his hand, he was ready to attack in order to demonstrate his impressive knowledge to us. His superiors lingered in the background, proud of their new wine expert whom they had trained up from the ground. We must have looked like an innocent and sheepish flock, compliant to our new master, willing to be wounded by his impressive knowledge. With each wine we realized more how little we knew and how much we needed this young

> *"That wine is of eternity
> I do not doubt;
> That wine might be
> crafted by angels
> Is perhaps also
> not a myth
> But those who drink
> it, whatever may be
> Gaze upon God's face
> with new vitality."*
>
> JOHANN WOLFGANG
> VON GOETHE
> (1749–1832),
> GERMAN POET

man to be our guide. A hierarchy had been established, and I saw that my encouragement to the guests to sense the wine for themselves fell on deaf ears. They were busy hunting for traces of smells and tastes that their master had enlightened them about. They had become compliant consumers and wanted to become "insiders."

The onslaught of information about each particular wine, its origin, the soil type, the grape variety, its regional particularity, its vintage, and the elaborate and detailed description about its flavor profile left our minds reeling. The young expert took captive our attention, and I am sure he did his very best to share his newly acquired knowledge and enlighten us. He spoke with authority and such assuredness. It was impressive. Wasn't the minerality of this wine astounding, and did the acidity not balance out the sweetness and fruit flavors well? Could we not smell the hints of apricot and stone fruit wafting out of the glass? Wasn't the wine well structured with a longish finish rounding up its composition elegantly?

As I looked around, I saw my guests frantically trying to process the highly technical language of the wine expert. The verbal torrents left their minds reeling as they were trying to process all the detailed information. At the same time, they were trying to sample the wine, to isolate smells and tastes and see if they matched up with the description of the expert. For the most part, the guests just nodded in confusion and stumbled along.

And I began to wonder what this way of presenting wine does to us. Yes, it can be incredibly enlightening, but I felt there was much that was getting lost. The guests couldn't hold all the information and process the sensations of the smell and taste of wine at the same time. The verbal onslaught was too powerful and blocked something within them. They lost trust in their own ability to encounter the wine, and they became obedient and compliant consumers in the presence of an "expert."

I felt that my spiritual exercise had failed. My wine pilgrims had shut down and lost confidence in their own sense of smell and taste. There was no way they could enjoy the fragrances of the wine, delight in its range of flavors, and be moved to a place of prayer and communion. It would take a lot of encouragement to help them feel confident again that they could enjoy wine on their own terms.

This experience made me realize that we need to reclaim wine as a gift from God for everyone. We can and should enjoy wine without the pressure to conform to this fairly young wine-speaking-and-writing guild. Too often they indulge in overuse of adjectives and adverbs to describe the wines, and scientific proof for their claims about the wine is sometimes lacking. This very particular way of presenting wine leaves little room for us to allow our own imagination to soar. An overly rationalized approach to wine locks us into a mental framework that is hard to climb out of. Choice wines can have a way with us that inspires us toward creativity, moves our emotions, opens us up to one another, and calls us into communion with God as we ponder his gifts with astonishment and wonder.

CHAPTER THIRTEEN

AWAKENING THE MUSE

Think not that Wine against good verse offends;
The Muse and Wine have been always friends.

JOHN MILTON

*T*hroughout the ages writers have emphasized that wine and the muse, the creative life, go together. From Homer to the author of the Song of Songs in the Bible, from Chaucer to Dante to Luther, from Shakespeare to Milton to Goethe, they all enjoyed a glass of wine while crafting their poetry. The Greek poet Homer wrote, "Wine is a magician, for it loosens the tongue and liberates good stories," and Martin Luther sipped Rhine wine while crafting his poetry.

Perhaps it seems strange to some that someone like the great Lutheran Reformer Martin Luther was sipping wine while writing the hymns that would capture his new theology and spread it among the common people and change the fate of Europe for good. But this is exactly what he did. Drunkenness is a dead-end road, but savoring wine with mindfulness and that slight sense of intoxication is perhaps more important to the creative process and the baptized imagination than we are ready to admit.

Some of you might feel a bit uneasy with the claim that wine can inspire creativity, especially if you have not grown up in a culture where wine was part of everyday life. What is it about wine that can inspire us? Is it its beauty, the alcohol, or the smell and taste of it? Most certainly all of them play some role. From a scientific perspective, the smell of wine seems to inspire the creative impulse in us. Neuroscientists in particular are researching how our brain processes smell and how this might affect our emotions and our memory. If the smell of wine somehow stirs our emotions and evokes memories, it can help loosen the creative impulse, as Homer wrote, and liberate us into creativity. The neurosciences are a fascinating field of research that challenges traditional understanding of how humans engage the world and respond to it. They point to a much more complex picture where all our senses are involved, including smell and taste.

> "When wine I quaff,
> before my eyes
> Drams of poetic
> glory rise;
> And freshened by
> the goblet's dews,
> My soul invokes the
> heavenly Muse."
>
> ANACREON
> (C. 582–485 BC),
> GREEK POET

A MORE HOLISTIC UNDERSTANDING

For the longest time we've had a fairly one-sided and hierarchical understanding of how we humans engage the world and how our different faculties work together. For the most part the church swallowed it hook, line, and sinker, and applied it to help us ingest spiritual truths. This is how it went: On the one hand we have the mind, that seemingly reliable and most "cognitive" and "objective" way to come to know things, followed by our will and then the "lower" faculties such as our emotions and our five senses. Obviously, theologians and philosophers have had quite varied understandings of what the *mind*, *will*, and *emotions* encompass, but the overall tendency was to prioritize the mind and the intellect. Within this framework the five senses still played an important role, but the senses of hearing (sermons and music) and seeing (reading and visual art) were considered most trustworthy for acquiring spiritual understanding. The senses of smell and taste were deemed dangerous for the pursuit of spiritual things, more likely to lead us astray rather than drawing us closer to God.

> "One thing a profound wine always does is to seize your imagination and hurl it a thousand feet into the air."
>
> TERRY THEISE,
> CONTEMPORARY
> AMERICAN WINE
> IMPORTER

This view of human beings, coupled with the effects of the Enlightenment and its emphasis on reason versus empiricism, led to an increasingly intellectualized approach to the Christian life, something that we still have not recovered from. Academic institutions in particular are often ridden by this tendency to intellectualize the Christian faith. Too often they leave students without the wisdom and the skills for living more balanced and integrated lives. How can healing and freedom come to our lives when ideas in our heads cannot penetrate into our guts, muscles, and bones, where the fears and agonies of long gone days seem to manifest themselves in anxious fright?

There are exceptions of course, but for the most part our professors and even pastors invite us to climb the ladder of intellectual ascent. They tend to leave other forms of explorations and expressions either to the psychologist or yoga teacher or relegate them to the church margins. Our cry for healing and wholeness is often left unanswered within the church.

There have always been movements that sought to correct this one-sided emphasis on the intellect, such as the great Romantic movement of the nineteenth century or more recently charismatic movements in the church. Looking back, however, the Romantic movement did not succeed in helping Western culture integrate into more wholesome ways of being in this world. Retreating back into the mind is always one easy way to feel safer and more secure, but in the end it leaves our emotional and spiritual lives shriveled and stifles our growth. In the broken and fractured world we inhabit, the challenge will always be how to find more integration, healing, and wholeness in our own lives that can then overflow into communities.

SMELLS, EMOTIONS, AND MEMORY

We now know that how we function as human beings is so much more complex than the categories of mind, will, and the lower faculties suggest. The only way we can come to know anything in the world is through our senses rather than through the mind that works magically apart from the senses. Our senses and our bodies more generally speaking are fundamental to our understanding of the world and are deeply and profoundly connected with one another and our body as a whole. They interact in subtle and wide-ranging ways and shape the way we experience the world around us. When we smell wine, for example, it can and will stir and move our emotions and memories without us even noticing it. Given the right context, atmosphere, and posture, savoring wine can stimulate us toward conversation and creativity not because of some magic but because our sense of smell affects us in such wide-ranging ways.

When we smell things, whether herbs from the garden or home-baked cookies or a glass of well-crafted wine, they often remind us of other things, memories and emotions we have stored in our bodies that are associated with those particular smells. I am sure you have experienced such connections.

Why would we want to single out wine as particularly evocative of long-held memories and emotions? Perhaps because wine can have such a wide range of different and subtle smells, it can tap into a wider range of memories and emotions and move us in more profound ways than other foods do.

It is easy and tempting to pass by this profound discovery of the neurosciences in relation to our sense of smell. It's easy to dismiss it as unimportant on the grand scale of theological inquiry and spiritual explorations. Let's pause here for a moment and take this in. Can we smell ourselves into remembering, feeling, and imagining things? And can we and should we draw on our sense of smell as we engage in spiritual practices? Can we reflect on the goodness of God as we attune our noses and tongues to a glass of well-crafted wine and learn to smell and taste the goodness of God in wine? Yes, we can, and it is quite biblical to do so. Think about the Lord's Supper. Jesus asked his disciples to eat bread and drink wine at the Passover meal turned into the Lord's Supper. As the disciples listened to Jesus' words, they chewed bread and savored multiple cups of wine. They sensed salvation in bread and wine.

For each of us this interaction between what we smell and taste in a wine and our memories and our emotions is a bit different. We pick up different things in a wine. What one person might perceive as blackberry smell in a wine will actually appear as a plum smell to someone else because they associate that particular smell with different memories and emotions stored in their body. And these smells evoke different emotions and memories in each one of us. If you have grown up in Asia, where your plants and foods smell quite different from the ones we have in the Western world, you will perceive the smells of wine in rather different terms. Your brain will associate the smell of wine with impressions stored by your particular cultural memory. That's why it is by far too restrictive and misleading to be too exact and precise when talking about wine flavors.

The more learned wine writers are, the more they will be aware of the limitations of language. They will be more careful about how to employ language to speak about wine. Wine writers such as Michael Broadbent, Andrew Jefford, and Karen MacNeil are perceptive and clear in their wine descriptions and yet make room for a more imaginative approach to wine. I've found them very helpful. They choose their metaphors for describing wine carefully to make sure that the readers' imagination can soar in between the lines of written explorations.

Unfortunately, most wine descriptions today are highly intellectualized in an attempt to be objective. Though never said out loud, the message underneath is that if you want to learn to taste wine properly, you will have to embrace and learn to excel in this particular way of tasting and talking about wine. It can easily reduce savoring wine into a straightjacket of hunting down seemingly exact flavor profiles. It squeezes the grandiose gift of wine into the narrow confines of tightly prescribed ways of how to talk about wine. Reason overrides emotions and memories and rules with a tight grip.

> *"Let us drink to have wit, not to destroy it."*
>
> CHARLES-FRANÇOIS PANARD
> (1689–1765), FRENCH POET

I am concerned that an overly intellectualized way of approaching wine can easily suffocate the imagination and stifle our emotional responses to wine. It does not do justice to what wine can and should do to us and with us. Wine is to stir our memories and our emotions and allow us to explore and engage the world in new, richer, and at times surprising ways.

WINE AND THE CREATIVE PROCESS

It takes creativity to craft beautiful wines, and beautiful wine can inspire creativity within us. They stir things within us that we can't even put into words. Beautiful wines move and delight us and beckon us to linger in the present moment, moments pregnant with meaning.

The process of becoming creative and allowing creative inspirations to arise within us can sometimes be a playful and light-hearted affair, but for the serious artist it is often a difficult and laborious journey. Distractions; battling inner demons like fear, self-doubt, and lack of confidence; or the sheer loneliness one faces as a creative are some of the small and great inner battles artistic people face.

The German poet Rainer Maria Rilke reflects on this creative process in his last sonnet of *Sonnets to Orpheus*. He writes:

> In the timberwork of the dark bell tower
> Allow yourself to be resounded.
> That which consumes you will become your strength
> What is your most painful experience?
> Is drinking from life's cup bitter, become wine.
> In this uncontainable night,
> be the mystery at the Calvary of your senses,
> Walk the Stations of the Cross
> In these strange encounters meaning arises from your senses.

Rilke encourages us to allow the creative wrestling and wrangling to do its work within us. He believes that our human senses have the way of the cross imprinted on them. Rilke does not explain what exactly he means by this, but this sonnet seems to suggest that if we welcome our creative agonizing and turmoil in light of Calvary and Christ's redemptive suffering, we will gain new strength and our creative struggles will be transformed into something beautiful. When life is bitter, he exclaims, allow it to turn into wine. For Rilke, the creative process, like fermentation, can transform mere water into delectable wine when we allow our suffering and agony to ferment into beauty.

It is perhaps the artist in our midst who is most prone to abuse alcohol in order to cope with the inner critic, the unpredictability of the creative process, and the uncertainty of the creative life. Some artists might be tempted to silence the inner critic by getting drunk, and therefore artists in particular must be careful not to abuse alcohol. When artists are embedded in a community, the community can and should help alleviate some of the struggles and challenges they face by providing companionship, shelter, and financial support.

People who follow the creative calling have different ways of dealing with the challenges and the demanding process that artistic expression takes. And yet there seem to be common threads people have followed to help cultivate the muse. The enjoyment of wine is one of them. Wine helps us to relax and let things flow, and its beautiful fragrance somehow stirs both memories and emotions and can liberate us to explore the not yet known.

> "If we sip the wine, we find dreams coming upon us out of the imminent night."
>
> D. H. LAWRENCE (1885–1930), ENGLISH POET AND NOVELIST

Beauty begets beauty. Who would not marvel at the deep, dark, red-purplish hues of a Syrah, when fragrances of dark berries and plums intermingle and dance together with the warmer scents hovering around memories of chocolate and cinnamon, allspice and vanilla? Ever so faint, other flavors come to the fore, echoing and singing and calling us to be still and listen and savor. And when we feel the rich, full, and strong juice of a Syrah glide over our tongues, it awakens our taste buds and our whole body seems to come alive. The wine makes our taste buds tingle. The alcohol and the tannins tease our most delicate and hidden cells like a passionate conductor, moving the symphony along our tongue, filling our whole mouth and throat with powerful sensations. What a marvelous experience it is when the heavy beauty of the wine gathers momentum to lift us to glorious culinary delights. It's easy to be swept away by such powerfully fragrant wines. Let go and be moved as faint memories come to the fore and feelings both familiar and long gone awaken you to the vision of new and hopeful things to come. And you will know in the depth of your soul that it is good to be here.

CHAPTER FOURTEEN

MUSINGS ON COMMUNITY FROM A WINE PILGRIM

Do not neglect to show hospitality to strangers, for by doing
that some have entertained angels without knowing it.

HEBREWS 13:2

I still remember vividly when I moved to the United States to begin my teaching job at a graduate school in Birmingham, Alabama. It was a big transition for me. It was my first teaching job in a new country and a new city, with a new culture to discover and learn. I spoke English fluently, but the subtleties of Southern culture cannot be learned quickly, nor are they apparent in plain language.

I had found a lovely place to live in the Highland Park area, a quiet neighborhood with old Southern homes that still had front porches and big balconies draped with sprawling tree branches. The neighborhood was a bit rundown, and the sidewalks were worn and cracked. I rented the top part of one of those old Southern homes. The wooden steps creaked as I walked upstairs, and the wooden floors were uneven. It had character, and I felt right at home there.

The kitchen was even smaller than my grandmother's had been, and the first piece of furniture I bought was a big oak table with matching chairs (from Craigslist) for the dining room. Still strapped from student days, I had little money to spare. Next came a swing and a little table for the balcony. I was in walking distance of a French bakery, the weekly farmer's market, and a supermarket called Piggly Wiggly, a funny name, I thought, for a supermarket. As I walked the aisles of the supermarket, I came upon the wine section. To my great delight, this small Piggly Wiggly carried wines from Franconia. The unique oval-shaped wine bottles filled with Silvaner wine felt like a warm welcome in a strange land. I couldn't believe my eyes when I saw those familiar bottles for sale so far away from home, as Franconian wines rarely make it into the international market.

For the first two months I slept on an air mattress as I waited for my belongings to arrive from Europe. A kind family, who had lived in the United Kingdom and returned home to Birmingham, knew what it was like to move to a new country and reached out to me through a mutual friend. They provided me with bedding, a pot, a pan, cups, plates, and cutlery. I was set with all the basics and ready to venture into a new season of life. A former professor of mine thought I might enjoy going to the Anglican cathedral, so on my first Sunday I hopped into my car and drove toward downtown. Being used to village and small-town life, I thought that somehow I would be able to find the cathedral easily. Little did I know.

As I was driving toward downtown, I found myself behind a sleek Mercedes-Benz station wagon. The lady at the wheel had a cute gray bob hairstyle, and it crossed my mind that she might be driving to church as well. So I followed her. Her name was Martha Ann Doyle, and she did drive to the cathedral to attend her first service there. We ended up sitting beside one another at church. It was only later that I found out that her husband had just passed away and it was too painful for her to return to the church she and her husband had attended most of their married life. Over the years an unlikely friendship developed. Martha Ann has taught me much about the South and its ways. Now in her mid-seventies, she is a woman full of zest for life and a mother to more than her two sons and daughters-in-law. She cared for her neighbor who had cancer and wrote wedding invitations for another neighbor's daughter. She is like a priest in disguise, listening, praying, and caring for those crossing her path. Her bereavement made her even more open and sympathetic to my own struggles of being a stranger in a foreign land.

Once I was more settled in my own home, Martha Ann would occasionally come over to my house on Saturdays. Busy as I was with teaching and writing, I had little energy left for much else, but I did manage to whip up the *New York Times*'s no-knead bread ingredients on Friday evening and bake it on Saturday morning.

With freshly baked bread, some smoked salmon from Piggly Wiggly, and a bottle of wine, we would sit on my balcony forging bonds of kinship over a small feast of bread and wine.

Martha Ann felt terribly intimidated by the world of wine, and it was one of my great delights to help her overcome her feelings of insecurity and intimidation. She hadn't grown up around wine and slowly learned what wines she really liked. As we sat on the swing in the shade of the tree branches and listened to the birds sing, she held her glass into the sky and began noticing colors, hues of gold and straw sparkling in the sunshine. She learned to swirl her glass gently and allow wafts of subtle aromas of fruit and floral delights to move her senses. She

> *"I was hungry and you gave me food, I was thirsty and you gave me something to drink, I was a stranger and you welcomed me."*
>
> MATTHEW 25:35

learned to move the wine around in her mouth and swallow the wine slowly so she could get the most out of each little sip. It was so fun to introduce her to a German Riesling and teach her to notice the subtle delights found in such a simple bottle of wine. These were glorious moments for us on my enchanting balcony. As Martha Ann moved through her season of grief and I adjusted to my new home and my new job, we grew closer to one another and closer to God, marveling at the wonders of what the earth can bring forth. We continue to savor the world together, allowing our hearts to swell and overflow with gratitude, knowing that life is fleeting and every moment counts.

Martha Ann wanted to know where she could find good quality wine that was in her budget, and I quickly realized that the local

Piggly Wiggly wasn't going to be the best option. So I started to explore and look around. I wanted to find a local wine shop with a good, wide selection of wines from Europe and the United States that Martha Ann would feel comfortable going to. It took me a while, but to my surprise I found a fantastic wine shop within five minutes' drive from my home. Tony, the owner, was quiet and reserved and did not overwhelm his customers with outlandish wine talk. He wasn't an outgoing, chatty man, and he reminded me more of my own Franconian culture. He was reserved and a bit on the grumpy side, but once I dug deeper, I discovered a man of knowledge and kindness for those who approached him as learners rather than wine snobs. He had a bit of a mixed reputation in town mainly because of his allergic reaction to arrogance of any kind. He had a fantastic selection of wines from Bordeaux and Oregon, wine regions I wanted to learn more about. To this day I believe that finding a good wine shop close to where we live is still the best way to discover the world of wine. It has the side effect of connecting us more to the community we live in.

My father made sure that I would not leave Germany without my annual allotment of wine. When my belongings, together with the wine, finally arrived in Birmingham, it was a great relief; I felt I could settle in more easily with all my humble possessions around me. Good wine is more expensive in the United States, and I had little spare money in my first year of teaching, so it was a great gift to have some Franconian wine stored in my air-conditioned dining room cupboard. My newly acquired oak table came with an extra leaf to extend for larger parties. With the wine glasses and plates unpacked, I was ready to welcome guests. I wasn't sure where I would get the energy to welcome guests and host dinner parties. My new teaching job took a lot out of me, and adjusting to a new culture was draining. A wise friend encouraged me to ask my guests to help and not put the burden on myself to do everything on my own. That's easier said than done for someone like me who wants to do it all and has a hard time asking for help. I am a slow learner. Asking for help became easier, and soon my apartment was filled with my students and new friends from a buzzing international community.

> *"Let all guests that happen to come be received as Christ, because He is going to say: 'A Guest was I and ye received Me.'"*
>
> **BENEDICT OF NURSIA (C. 480–C. 543), AUTHOR OF THE RULE OF ST. BENEDICT**

DISCOVERING THE FEAST

One of the courses I taught at graduate school was an introduction to Christian spirituality. The course climaxed in exploring hospitality as a spiritual practice. I had my students watch two films, *Avalon* and *Babette's Feast*. *Avalon* tells the story of the disappearance of table fellowship in American family life, and *Babette's Feast* tells the story of the recovery of the table and convivial celebration in an uptight, guilt-ridden, and melancholic Lutheran sect. I had all of my students over for a meal to celebrate the end of the semester, and of course I served wine.

My students were a bit older and as far as I could tell not really into binge drinking. For the most part they were serious and hard-working. I remember one of my students in particular. He had come from a long tradition of horseshoers, wore cowboy boots, played the banjo, and in his spare time went to play music at different venues. He seemed exotic to me, from a world I knew little of. He had come to seminary to do serious theological study, and I could tell he felt uncomfortable in my class. As the atmosphere got more relaxed around food and wine, he became a bit more talkative and told me that his wife would like my class. Having learned enough about Southern culture, I could tell that was his way of saying he did not love my class and didn't know what to do with my teaching. He wanted serious academic studies to prepare him and his wife to become missionaries in India. Perhaps my insistence on the importance of simple practices like hospitality threw him a bit off-kilter. I really don't know. He soon disappeared into the fog of rigorous academic study and emerged three years later in my class on the history of the care and cure of souls. There was no way for him around this required class.

At the end of the semester, I once again had the class over to my place. It was the beginning of May, and we sat outside on the balcony, the sun setting over downtown Birmingham. The heat had come back, and cicadas were chirping their song in unison. My students were munching on chips and salsa, sipping glasses of sparkling wine, obviously relieved that the end of the semester had come. My exotic horseshoer had brought his wife along, and they were sitting on my swing, relaxed, enjoying the leisurely pace of the evening. I hadn't talked to him and was eager to hear about their plans as he was finishing his studies. To my great surprise, they had changed their plans. They no longer wanted to become missionaries in India. A new vision for life in their homeland had grown over time. He wanted to return to practice horseshoeing part time with his father and take on a small parish in rural Alabama. They wanted to create a home of hospitality where they could open their doors and invite a hurting world to find a place to heal. I was moved to tears but held back and just marveled.

THE LORD'S SUPPER AND HOSPITALITY

We live in unsettling times. It's tempting for me to give in to despair and fear of what is to come. The daily news only exacerbates those feelings. Good news doesn't seem to come through the news channels anymore. Where do I cultivate hope and joy? Every Sunday I walk up to the altar to receive bread and wine in celebration of the Lord's Supper.

Every Sunday I taste the goodness of God as wine makes my taste buds tingle and warms my body as I swallow it slowly. This wonderful and mysterious ritual calls me to leave behind my fears and worries about what is to come and trust that God has not abandoned this world. God woos us like a lover woos his bride to come and make our home with him. Christ comes with healing in his wings to redeem, to restore, and to make whole. As I hold out my hands, cupped to receive the bread, and as I take a generous gulp of wine from the chalice, I remember and embrace this hope.

Somehow we are called to become part of this great mystery, enlivened and refreshed by the reviving power of God's Spirit, who invites us to join in and reach out into a broken world.

I didn't always feel like opening my home to welcome guests. Sometimes I just wanted to turn in on myself and allow the loneliness to overtake me and feel sorry for myself. Loneliness is real and can eat away at our souls like rust without us even noticing it. Mother Teresa once said that loneliness is the leprosy of the West. Every time has its own challenges, and one of the greatest challenges of our time is the isolation and loneliness many of us experience. To reach out and draw people out of their isolation is one of the great callings of our time.

My big oak table from Craigslist could easily sit eight, but with the leaf inserted I was able to squeeze twelve around the table. Many times I pushed the table to the wall and turned the party into a buffet-style evening. I provided some wine, baked bread, and made an easy chicken dish or a pasta salad, simple food really. My guests would bring more dishes, more wine, and some desserts, and in no time we had a feast going. I liked to light candles in the dining room, the hallway, the living room, and on the balcony. It made the whole apartment more inviting and gave it a lovely and warm glow. With a glass of wine and

> *"The juice of the grape is given to him that will use it wisely, as that which cheers the heart of man after toil, refreshes him in sickness and comforts him in sorrow. He who so enjoyeth it may thank God for his wine-cup as for his daily bread; and he who abuseth the gift of heaven is not a greater fool in his intoxication than thou in thine abstinence."*
>
> SIR WALTER SCOTT
> (1771–1832),
> SCOTTISH NOVELIST,
> POET, AND HISTORIAN

a plate of food in hand, my guests would spread out and settle in different parts of my home. As people lingered and sipped their wine, their conversations would become more animated and lively. Laughter would fill the home, and some turned to serious conversations. The sound of togetherness would resonate through the house, and a deep feeling of satisfaction would come over me. As the evening came to a close, I liked to move to the balcony, sit on the swing, and listen to the cicadas. The stars would sparkle over Birmingham as I took another sip of our fresh and crisp Silvaner, cooling me off and calming me down after a busy evening of tending to my guests.

It doesn't take much to create a little feast and cultivate the power of conviviality in your midst. If nothing else, I hope you feel liberated to put a little food together and a simple but well-crafted bottle of wine. It's not about creating the perfect feast. It's about welcoming guests into your life even and perhaps precisely when you don't feel like you have it all altogether. We all share similar journeys, perhaps at different times in our lives, and to do it well we need to walk this journey together. A bottle of wine shared around the dinner table will help create a festive atmosphere and unleash the power of conviviality in your midst. The beauty of the wine will remind you of the goodness of God. As you linger, you can savor yourselves into soulful celebrations. Don't be afraid to let go and be overtaken by a festive spirit, for God gave wine to make glad our hearts. Wine is God's way of kissing humanity. Let's savor his goodness toward us.

WINE AS A BLESSING

May God give you of the dew of heaven,
and of the fatness of the earth,
and plenty of grain and wine.

Isaac blesses Jacob, Genesis 27:28

*I*t really came as a surprise to me when I first stumbled across a passage in the Bible that suggested that wine is a blessing from God. I hadn't thought that much about what a blessing actually means other than that it somehow connects us to God and his benevolence toward us. People say they are blessed with good health and good friends or with children and a successful career. Whether they think that God might be involved in all of this is perhaps another matter altogether.

Growing up in the Lutheran Church, the pastor, with quite dramatic posture and voice, would always say a blessing over the congregation: "The Lord bless you and keep you: the Lord make his face shine upon you, and be gracious to you; the Lord lift up his countenance upon you, and give you peace." While saying the prayer, he would raise his hands slowly and make the sign of the cross over the congregation. This dramatic moment at the end of the service felt like a good omen to me. It was comforting to know that God would be with me, protect me, be gracious to me, and give me peace. I loved those words spoken over us every Sunday, and I had no clue that they were taken from the Old Testament. God's blessing, I figured, was a sort of immaterial, comforting, and reassuring knowledge that God was there. Little did I know.

In Genesis, the first book of the Bible, blessings are important, and they are directly linked to God's action in this world. As God calls people and sends them forth, he blesses them so they can be a blessing to others. God's blessing is not a general "we wish you well in God's name" but a dynamic gift that we must not hoard, store, and stack away but share with the world.

Wine is a special gift from God and part of God's mission in this world. That's why Jesus' first miracle was turning water into wine. God's blessing was upon this man, and through him God's mission would continue.

What then is wine for? In its most profound sense, wine is a gift from God and a tangible blessing. It's a material sign of God's benevolence that is to soften the hard places within us and make us more receptive toward God and (for)giving toward one another. Few have ventured forth to reflect on this mysterious quality of wine as a blessing. Perhaps it blurs too much the boundaries between heaven and earth, the sacred and the secular, the material and immaterial, the severe and the joyful. Wine as a blessing invites us to live with these tensions and not dissolve them too easily until we learn to inhabit both worlds with grace and joy.

May you be blessed as you explore what it means that wine is a gift and blessing from God. And as you share this mysterious gift with those God places into your path, may a convivial spirit draw you closer to him from whom all true blessings flow.

GRATITUDE

*T*his book emerged out of the complex terroir of growing up on a family-run winery, my personal search for a wholesome and healing Christian spirituality, and my professional life as a theologian. Growing up on a winery informed this book as much as my now thirty-year-long search for a more holistic, embodied, and communal Christian spirituality. I would like to close this book with a profound sense of gratitude for the sun and soil, rain and wind, colleagues, friends, and family who have provided the rich terroir for this book to emerge and ripen into fruition.

After the release of my book *The Spirituality of Wine* in 2013, I went on an extensive book tour. I am especially grateful to Steven and Amy Purcell and Steve and Nancye Drukker for their hospitality in the beautiful Texas Hill Country as I was getting ready to venture forth on this book tour. Whilst sipping some lovely Texas wines, Amy, Nancye, and I felt inspired and brainstormed together ideas for a new book—this book. Amy and Nancye's encouragement to develop my work for a wider readership has been the sun and soil for a new vintage. Thank you for nudging me in this direction.

Since then I have literally traveled around the globe to offer events around the subject of the spirituality of wine and lead my guests into wine tasting as a spiritual practice. Many have contributed with questions, comments, and new insights. Though I cannot name everybody here, I am so grateful for your support and hospitality, the conversations we've had, and the insights I have received as we continue to explore what it means to receive wine as a gift from God. Thank you to Bill and Nancy Carroll, Angela Ferguson, Doris Mobley, Helen and Devin Dolive, Julie and Howard McKay, Richard and Janet Vest, Roy Smith, Jack Evans, Glenda Curry, Charlotte Ann Adams, Kristen Deede Johnston, Amy Ruis, Gordon Fee, Cherith Fee-Nordling, Alice and Chris Canlis, Chelle Sterns, Tim Oas, Stuart McNight, Jacquie and Dave Smyth, Charlene and Peter Sanctucci, Russ Raney, Scot Sherman, Kyle Logan, Susie Lipps, Kermit Lynch, Tim Mondavi, Peter Brown, Nathan Stucky, Peter and Miranda Harris, and Matthias Wagner. Thank you especially for the folks in New Zealand and Hong Kong: Mark Johnston and Carolyn Kelly, Alan Brady, Steve Taylor, and Benedict Ng. Mike Summerfield and Noranne Ellis have been especially important to me and this book as they gave me encouragement and feedback, and shared my passion for the gift of wine. I cannot thank enough my editor, Cindy Bunch, at InterVarsity Press for sharing my vision and her willingness to take on this project. Her thoughtful insights have made this book flow much more smoothly.

My family continues to be busy running the family winery and they welcome me back whenever I show up on their doorstep, ready to uncork a bottle of wine in joyful reunion. Dad continues to send me steady supplies of wine. Thank you for your generosity in spirit and wine.

HOW TO SAVOR
WINE SOULFULLY

*W*ine is an affair of the heart. Savoring wine can and should be an affair of the heart where we are moved and touched and elevated. We need to reclaim wine as a gift from God, a gift that is to bring us closer to one another, to the earth, and ultimately to the Giver of all good gifts, God himself. That's why I think it is important to begin savoring wine with a posture of gratitude and the sound of thanksgiving and togetherness.

INSTRUCTIONS FOR THE SEVEN SENSES

Sound: The clinking of glasses is the sound of togetherness. The rituals we surround ourselves with tell us much about who we are and what we value. As you open a bottle of wine, listen to the sound as the wine is uncorked. It's a lovely sound. As the cork slowly glides along the inside of the bottleneck and as it finally makes its escape, it pops out with a great sigh of relief. It is a lovely sound. Unscrewing a screw cap does not quite cut it, but it's still worth listening to. Then pour the wine into the glass. The glug-glug sounds of pouring not only ring nicely in the ear, but they also tell your brain to awaken your taste buds. It's time to arise from the slumber and get ready for the pleasures to come. In German we have a name for it: *Vorfreude*—"anticipatory joy." You are now ready for the ritual.

Since ancient times people have made toasts before drinking wine. When everybody has a glass of wine in hand, raise it heavenward to give thanks to God our heavenly Father for his lavish generosity. Then clink your wine glasses with one another as a sign of reconciliation and good will. As you do this, look one another in the eyes. Where I come from it is the rule and custom (we Germans thrive on rules and customs) to look into the eyes of the other as your glasses clink. Now that takes some practice because you need to direct your glass with your eyes and hands to the glass of the other. You can do a bit of back and forth with your eyes, but as the glasses clink you must have your eyes firmly fixed on the eyes of the other. This is important. It is here that the bonds of togetherness receive their first seal. Allow the sound of the clinking of the wine glasses to resound in your ears as you continue to behold the other. Sight and sound seal the moment of communal bonding. Stay in the moment and don't rush off too quickly. Rituals matter. Only now are you ready to approach the wine with due reverence.

Sight: The hues and depth of colors and the flow of fluids (viscosity). You can now direct your attention toward the wine in the glass. Hold the glass at a good distance. Notice the color of the wine, the depth of the color, and the range of hues. It's easier to notice the different hues of a wine when you hold it against a white tablecloth but don't get too fuzzed over it. In a white wine you might discover hues of straw with glimpses of green or silver, or perhaps the wine is golden or even slightly orange. Does it remind you of a sunny day, a drizzle of rain, or drops from a honeycomb? In a red wine the range of colors might reach from light pink to purple to reddish brown to dark dirt. What depth do the colors have?

It is quite remarkable what a glorious array of colors and hues wines can have, whispers from a master painter who delights to make this world a colorful place. As you tilt the glass a little, continue to enjoy the color and delight in the range of hues found from the edge to the center of the wine glass. Small things matter, and color is no small matter. Now begin to gently swirl the wine in the glass and watch the movement. Does the wine seem on the thinner side or does it seem thick or even oily? The wine's viscosity is no sign of quality but helps to understand the wine. Wines with higher sugar and alcohol content are heavier and form those "legs" on the side of the wine glass. Swirl the wine once more and it is time to draw nearer to that blessed beverage.

Smell: The wafts of aroma. Gently raise the glass to your nose and allow the wafts of aromas to stir you. Noticing smells, especially subtle smells, takes time. Relax your posture, lower the glass, and ponder. Swirl the wine in the glass once more, and take another sniff and sit with it. What does the smell remind you of? Do this repeatedly, but don't rush. Most of what we think is the taste of a wine is actually its aroma. Treasures abound but most of them are subtle and discreet; some of them can't be captured in words at all.

Do the aromas remind you of particular fruits or herbs or floral scents? Perhaps the wine reminds you of the rich smell of spices, oak, or even earth freshly scooped from the ground. Some wines only unfold their aroma over time, others have little, and still others have astonishing complexity. As a novice you might find some smells in wine even repelling. Notice the smells and commit them to memory. Allow the smells to evoke feelings and memories and inspire your conversations and musings. Trust your instincts as you search for words to match your findings. Sit with the aromas and savor them; they are good company and work wonders to revitalize your tired brain cells.

Taste: Teasing your taste buds. Now it's time to take a sip of wine from the glass, and if possible draw in some air with the wine. It will help unfold the flavors of the wine. Move the wine around in your mouth and let it slowly glide over your tongue and taste buds. Be playful and patient, and don't swallow the wine too quickly. Let it sit in your mouth for a good while. As the wine warms and mingles with your saliva, you will notice how the wine unfolds its taste and releases more of its aroma through the retronasal passage. It's a complex process and all you need to do is "listen" and turn your attention toward the wonders unfolding in your mouth.

Does the wine taste sweet or dry? Does the acidity (a kind of sour or tart taste) taste sharp, or is it like background music, soft and gentle? Chardonnays from Chablis tend to have a high amount of acidity. The tannins in red wine can feel a bit abrasive, like sandpaper or dryness on your tongue. Are the tannins irritatingly brash or just gently teasing your taste buds? Cabernet Sauvignons, Syrahs, and Nebbiolos tend to be high in tannins. With time tannins tend to become mellower and at their best blend into the wine. Can you taste distinct fruit flavors, or does the wine have a buttery creaminess to it?

As you slowly swallow the wine, taste and smell integrate and leave a fuller impression. That's why it is important to continue to pay attention even as you swallow the wine: you are still smelling the wine through your retronasal passage!

In wine we literally taste and see the goodness of God as he blesses us with such abundant gifts of manifold flavors. Enjoy them even though you might not be able to put them into words. Grunts and sighs of gratitude will do. God knows and will receive them with pleasure.

Touch: Feeling the body and structure. From the time wine touches our lips to feeling the wine on our tongue, on the tender skin of the roof of our mouth, and inside our cheeks, and as we swallow the wine and it glides down our throat, we can feel the touch of wine. Lighter wines will feel more like a gentle brush of wind while strong red wines high in alcohol will feel heavy and perhaps even imposing, reverberating through our bodies.

Wines have texture and structure, and the acidity of the wine helps build structure in a wine. The right balance between acidity, sugar, and alcohol are basic plumb lines, the scaffolding that holds the wine together. All the other impressions of color, viscosity, smell, and taste find their place in that structure, sometimes well integrated and in harmony with one another, sometime awkwardly layered and out of tune. I've always wondered whether medieval monks sought to build a cathedral structure into their wines, allowing them to host a symphonic presence that would move the attentive drinker to a place of wonder. With time, you will be able to recognize whether a wine is well structured and crafted like a symphony, trickles along like bland elevator music, or surprises you with new compositions that challenge the traditional palate.

Inner awareness: Responding to the wine. It's quite deceptive to think that we have only five senses. We all have an inner sense that helps us be in touch with our bodies and how we feel inside our own skin. With this inner sense we respond to impressions we receive from the outside world. Once we have an impression of a given wine, we will respond to it whether we are aware of it or not. As the wine enlivens our five senses, stirs our emotions, and reawakens certain memories, we can allow the wine to move us. Give yourself permission to respond to the wine more fully, not just with judgment but with musings, laughter, or even tears.

An unpleasant and uneven wine might irritate us in subtle ways, stifle our imagination and the conversations we are having around the table. A beautiful wine will likely do the opposite: it will awaken and enliven our inner sense, open us up, and inspire our musings and conversations. All of this might happen quite naturally, without you being aware of it, but these impressions and musings are an important part of savoring wine. Don't be shy; allow yourself to be carried away a little.

I vividly remember talking to a well-known vintner in Oregon. He is weary about how many talk about wine these days, especially in the journalistic arena. He now judges a wine by what it does to him. The wine was good and perhaps even excellent if it has enriched his conversations with his wife around the dinner table. It's that simple for him. The bonds of kinship continue to be strengthened and sealed as we savor wine together and allow it to resound in and among us.

Soul: Soulful savoring. It's striking to me that many Christians don't seem to savor the wine they drink from the chalice in the Lord's Supper. Perhaps it's just not good wine, or they don't get

enough of it to really taste it properly. It's as if a deep-seated ambivalence continues to haunt us and keep us from communing with
God through this precious gift of wine in the Eucharist. This is
where we need to have a conversion experience. We must turn all
of our senses, including our senses of smell, taste, and touch, toward
the cup as we embrace that great mystery we receive in bread and
wine. Can we allow the God of all creation to liberate us into a
more sensual experience of the Lord's Supper? Can we make room
for our noses and tongues to sense salvation as the wine tingles on
our lips, teases our taste buds, and warms our bodies?

Next time you partake in the Lord's Supper, make sure you get
a good gulp of wine to ensure that you have a good tasting experience. I know that is not always easy. I vividly remember our new
rector who thought that a tiny sip was just enough to do the job. It
didn't do it for me. I wanted more. And the congregation didn't
agree with him either. We all wanted more. We wanted to experience the generosity of God in a generous sip from the Eucharistic
cup. So we made our needs known. Our pastor is now less
controlling when he holds the chalice and allows us to drink more
deeply from the sacred cup. What a relief and what a gift!

But that is only the beginning. From this ritual of the Lord's
Supper we now see the world with new eyes, with visions of redemption and reconciliation in our midst. Every meal and every
bottle of wine shared around the dinner table can now become an
extension of the Lord's Supper where we sense God's presence with
us. It is here that we can embrace and cultivate a more soulful way
of savoring—allowing our souls to swell in gratitude, joy, and
anticipation as we sense Emmanuel, God with us.

DISCUSSION GUIDE
AND WINE TASTING TIPS

*H*ere are some questions for reflection. You can journal about them or discuss them with a group. Focus on those questions and practices that seem most helpful to you.

Pair them with a wine tasting and it will make this into a more full-bodied experience.

WINE TASTING TIPS

With each session, I suggest you sample two to three different wines and savor them alongside one another as you discuss the questions. The learning curve will be much higher when you sample more than one wine and compare them to one another. These wines can be of the same grape variety from different regions (like Cabernet Sauvignon from California, the South of France, and Australia), or three different grape varieties like a Chardonnay, Pinot Gris, and a Riesling. If you come from a wine region or have a wine region close by, why not start locally and try some local wines?

Where should you buy wine? You can go to your local wine shop, ask at a local restaurant with a good wine list where to shop for well-crafted wine, or try to find a good wine shop online. I prefer to go to my local wine shop because it has the added benefit of meeting other local wine lovers who shop there, and I like to support family-run businesses. Be clear about your budget and communicate it well in advance of your purchase. My experience is that a good wine shop will always give you a better deal for your money than a supermarket.

Create a little sanctuary to savor wine: turn off music; remove any items with a strong smell such as flowers, scented candles, and so forth; and keep things visually simple so you can actually focus on the wine and not be distracted. Read through my instructions on how to savor wine soulfully, and keep a journal to make some notes. Make sure you have enough time on hand so you don't have to rush through the wines or the questions. I recommend at least one hour per session; two would be better. Allow some silence while you sample the wines and to ponder their aroma.

SESSION 1: WINE AS A GIFT FROM GOD
Chapters 1-4

- Wine is the most talked about food in the Bible. In recent history, theologians and pastors have paid little attention to it. Why do you think that is?

- What did your family of origin teach you about wine?

- What does your church teach about wine and the gifts of the earth more generally speaking?

- How do you feel about wine?

- The Psalms teach us that God gave wine to bring us joy. How do you feel about receiving joy as a gift from God and the cultivation of joy as an important spiritual practice?

- The earth and the fruit it brings forth are part of God's good creation. Do you find it difficult to view what grows on the earth as an expression of God's love?

- What practices might help you to connect to God through the gifts of the earth, including wine?

- Do you find it easy to identify your emotional and spiritual thirst, and how do you tend to quench it?

- What practices might help you get in touch and keep in touch with your deeper thirsts and learn to quench them in wholesome ways?

- Have you ever felt God's touch while enjoying something special like an amazing meal, a beautiful wine, or strolling through a garden?

SESSION 2: COMING HOME— SENSING SALVATION
Chapters 5-7

- What does *home* mean to you? Does a sense of place play into it?

- Do you feel a strong connection to a particular place, and is it somehow related to the food that is grown there?

- We are often unaware of how our lack of connection to place affects us. Do you think you are affected by it? In what way?

- What practices would help you feel more connected to the place where you live and to the earth more generally speaking?

- Well-crafted wines can reflect the particular places where they come from. Have you ever tasted such a wine, and did it stir longings in you? If so, what?

- The Garden of Eden in Genesis literally means the garden of "delight and pleasure." How do you feel about relating to God through the sensual delights and pleasures of food and wine?

- What is your relationship with food and wine? Does it need healing?

- How do you feel about your senses of touch, smell, and taste? Are they strongly developed senses? If not, why?

- Do you actually smell and taste the wine served at the Lord's Supper? Does it help you ingest spiritual realties?

- What rituals would help you cultivate savoring food and wine as a spiritual practice, a form of prayer?

SESSION 3: WINE AND EVERYDAY SPIRITUALITY

Chapters 8-11

- The joy we receive from wine is joy that has grown through the wine press. How is pursuing immediate pleasure different from cultivating joy? How might this affect the way you drink wine?

- To learn to savor is a journey. How can you expand your smelling and tasting experience in daily life?

- What are some of the flavors you enjoy? What smells and tastes give you pleasure?

- What memories if any do you have of your family feasting together? Are they happy memories or sad or painful? Are you in need of healing in this regard?

- What practices can you cultivate to make feasting a regular occurrence in your home? What keeps you from doing it, and what are the challenges involved?

- Are you feeling intimidated by the thought of having people over and sharing a bottle of wine with them? If so, how could you learn to overcome those feelings?

- How can you be at ease with an imperfect home and an imperfect self, and focus on the grace that is in a bottle of well-crafted wine, embracing God's love and grace as you host people in your home?

- How can you rid yourself of perfectionism in regard to hospitality and allow things to be simple?

- What thoughts do you have about wine, sex, and God?

- Wine brings comfort to the aging. What comforts do the elderly in your family have? Why not share a glass of wine with them once in a while?

SESSION 4: THE FREEDOM TO ENJOY WINE AND SENSUAL WORSHIP

Chapters 12-14

- How do you respond when you walk into a wine shop or listen to a wine expert talk about wine? Is it helpful, overwhelming, or confusing?

- Do you feel easily intimidated by wine and the wine world?

- What can you do to overcome any feelings of intimidation and be free to explore wine on your own terms?

ᕦᕤ It's tempting to not pay attention to the wine in your glass and just focus on conversations. Why not take a few minutes and practice paying attention to the subtle aromas in the wine in your group?

ᕦᕤ Write down what you smell and taste and sense and feel. This might help you pay attention. Allow things to flow. Welcome the muse.

ᕦᕤ As you explore the wine, send a thought of gratitude to God.

ᕦᕤ Pause and remember that life, despite all its challenges, is a gift from God.

ᕦᕤ Wine is meant to be shared. In the next month or so, think of one or two friends who might be lonely and invite them over for a glass of wine and draw them into a wine tasting experience. Enjoy the journey of learning about wine together.

ᕦᕤ Next time you partake in the Lord's Supper, take a big gulp of wine. Try to smell and taste it, and savor this moment of remembrance with your nose and tongue.

ᕦᕤ Continue this moment of remembrance at home and celebrate Sunday with your loved ones with a bottle of well-crafted wine. Embrace resting in the arms of God. Be joyful.

NOTES

CHAPTER 2: A JOYFUL JOURNEY
TO A SPIRITUAL GIFT

p. 13   *deeply flawed approach to the spiritual life*: For a careful discussion of this including how to deal with alcohol abuse see my book *The Spirituality of Wine* (Grand Rapids: Eerdmans, 2016), chap. 9.

CHAPTER 6: MAKING PEACE
WITH WINE AND FOOD

p. 48   *Those who struggle with alcohol addiction*: See my chapter "Wine and the Abuse of Alcohol" in *The Spirituality of Wine* (Grand Rapids: Eerdmans, 2016) for a careful discussion of this important concern.

p. 49   *Last evening I was at a graduation ceremony*: Personal email correspondence, September 22, 2017. Used with permission.

CHAPTER 8: LEARNING ABOUT
JOY FROM THE WINE PRESS

p. 75   *making love only for the moment of orgasm*: This analogy was inspired by an analogy made by Stephen Nachmanovitch, *Free Play: Improvisation in Life and Art* (New York: Penguin, 1990), 18.

CHAPTER 11: WINE, HEALTH, AND HEALING

p. 101   *cardiovascular diseases are the leading cause of death*: For more detailed information and references to a meta-analysis on this topic, see my book *The Spirituality of Wine* (Grand Rapids: Eerdmans, 2016), 176-78. Wine consumed more than in moderation can slightly increase the risk of some cancers such as breast cancer in women.

CHAPTER 13: AWAKENING THE MUSE

p. 116   *Think not that Wine against good verse offends*: John Milton, *Elegy VI: To Charles Diodati, When He Was Visiting in the Country*. I have replaced Milton's "The Muse and Bacchus" with "The Muse and Wine" in order to clarify the meaning.

p. 121   *They sensed salvation in bread and wine*: For a more detailed exploration of how this works, see my chapter "Wine in the Lord's Supper: Christ Present in Wine," in *The Spirituality of Wine* (Grand Rapids: Eerdmans, 2016).

p. 123   *In the timberwork of the dark bell tower*: Rainer Maria Rilke, *Duineser Elegien: Die Sonette an Orpheus* (Wiesbaden: Insel Verlag, 1949), my translation.

p. 123   *For Rilke, the creative process*: Many translators think that the German word *Kreuzweg* means "crossroads" in English, but that is incorrect. It means "the way of the cross" or "Stations of the Cross." The German word for "crossroads" is *Kreuzung*.